Think Right, Feel Right

*The Building Block Guide for Happiness
and Emotional Well-being*

Think Right, Feel Right

The Building Block Guide for Happiness

and Emotional Well-being

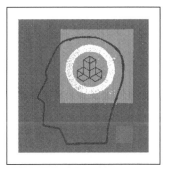

Robert D. Isett, Ph.D.

In memory of Edward Querner, whose

loving spirit graced so many lives

Contents

how we think and feel

Preface

To flourish, all living things need proper care. Imagine if we planted a garden and simply left it to grow on its own without watering, weeding, or any cultivation. Our garden would perish rather than flourish. As you will see, the same is true for us.

Unfortunately, many of us have not learned how to nurture ourselves adequately: we struggle to find happiness and emotional well-being[1], unable to garner the nurturance we need from within ourselves or from the world around us. For many, peace and happiness seem situational and fleeting. In this game of emotional lottery, our winnings are hard to hold onto, forever being won and then lost by life's ups and downs.

Now you are about to learn how to overcome the pitfalls that vanquish so many and hold onto the well-being you create. By reading this book, you will embark on a very positive and powerful life-changing journey. This will not be a wasted journey through empty platitudes that merely list what you should be doing, but instead a journey that really shows and teaches you what to do and how to do it. You are about to discover how to

---

[1]For the purposes of this book, emotional well-being is an inclusive term reflecting the ability to be: 1) self-esteeming, 2) peaceful, 3) free of emotional symptoms, and 4) happy. Some examples of emotional symptoms are persistent guilt, anger, depression, worry, anxiousness, misuse of drugs or alcohol. When this ability is at its highest level, well-being will also be highest. Conversely, mental well-being will be low when this ability is low.

put yourself, rather than circumstance, in charge of your own nurturance and emotional well-being. You are about to add deeper and more lasting joy to your life.

The guide is a genuine and informative "how-to" handbook for understanding how your emotions work and learning how to develop happiness as part of your daily routine. Admittedly, we already have a host of self-help and academic books in the marketplace that address different aspects of self-esteem, happiness, and well-being from varying perspectives. However, none of these books offer us a complete, step-by-step approach that fully explains what these vital emotional resources are, or precisely how we go about developing them. This book does.

Written with a common sense feel, the guide is logical, practical, and easy to follow. It will show you how to permanently feel better about yourself and the world around you. The guide's clear and readable style is well-suited to both the adult and young adult general readership.

The methods and concepts contained in the guide represent innovations I have developed and tested over many years in private practice. They are tools rooted in the thinking of Cognitive Behavioral Therapy[2] as well as the emergent influences of Positive Psychology. Using the methods described in detail throughout this book, I have spent more than two decades successfully teaching clients how to eliminate emotional upsets and disturbances, conquer persistent and disabling emotional

---

[2]Cognitive Behavioral Therapy is a general term for psychotherapies that focus on modifying thinking to improve psychological functioning and emotional health. Positive Psychology is a relatively new branch of psychology that seeks to understand and promote emotional well-being.

disorders, build stronger self-esteem, and experience deeper emotional well-being. By learning and implementing a cognitive behavioral model that promotes optimal emotional functioning and self-nurturance, my clients regularly show sustained improvements in personal happiness as well as symptom reduction. By dedicating yourself to gaining the knowledge contained in this book, you too can realize these benefits.

For many people, happiness is by no means a guarantee. Some of us seem to have a lot of it, some very little and a lot of us are happy just some of the time. Many people implicitly think that joy and contentment will result from having the right possessions and circumstances in life. This assumption may be true in one sense: when these possessions and circumstances are present, we feel good for a time, however, when circumstances change or time passes, we lose those good feelings. Following these avenues to well-being, our happiness is intermittent and event-based, rather than sustained and internally driven. We believe that Things[3] cause us to feel happy, but in their absence we become upset and disturbed because these Things are no longer around to support us. Many of us spend a lot of time and money trying to get Things and make Things right so we feel good. In doing so, we mistakenly assign the causes of our feelings to external events, rather than to our thoughts about these events. In other words, we become "situation-bound", waiting for periodic happiness to come our

---

[3] "Thing" is used as a capitalized word throughout this book when referring to circumstances or events that we assume cause our feeling states. In the statement, "That movie will make you sad," movie is an example of a Thing.

way. Because we can't always control situations, we are likely to feel that our happiness is often out of our direct control: if this is how we have learned to think about happiness, it is.

Many of us find ourselves struggling with intermittent mood swings, bouts of depression, stress, outbursts of anger, road rage, worry, anxiety, low self-esteem, and other emotional issues. We want to feel better, but we may not have a clear picture of what we need to do, or not do, to make this happen. In an effort to make our lives feel better, we compensate by overeating, abusing alcohol, becoming addicted to work, overspending, or through some other problematic behavior.

As important as emotional wellness is to both our mental and physical health, the knowledge most of us have about emotional wellness and happiness is often limited to the hit-or-miss learning afforded by life experience and happenstance. Because emotional learning is so closely tied to the capriciousness of life circumstances, there is no guarantee that we will learn the right and essential emotional knowledge to be happy and emotionally well. Many of us reach adulthood without receiving any formal education regarding what emotions are, or what causes them. Without this teaching, we go through life lacking a full understanding of what we should do to assess and change our emotions or best regulate how we feel.

When, if ever, during our formal education were we actually given the opportunity to learn the specifics of happiness or taught how to go about giving ourselves more lasting well-being? We were taught and tested on the state capitals, multiplication tables, long division, parts of speech and periodic elements, but never taught or tested on happiness or emotional well-being. To feel well and stay that way, we must know how our emotions work and how to maintain sound emotional health and well-being. In reading the guide, you will now gain important emotional knowledge for improved happiness and emotional health.

As you read this book, you will learn how your emotions work, how you can change them to improve how you feel, and how you can achieve more sustainable happiness. In a logical, step-by step fashion, this book guides you through a series of highly instructional "Building Blocks" which will widen and deepen your understanding of many important topics, including:

> ➤ The role of thinking in emotions
> ➤ The types of thinking that cause positive and negative emotions
> ➤ Correct use of your thinking and emotions to optimize well-being
> ➤ Developmental factors that promote and impair optimal emotional learning
> ➤ And essential techniques for changing and better controlling how you feel

Once you have completed the first seven Building Blocks, you will build upon this foundational learning. You will complete an exercise that clarifies the essential elements for emotional well-being and assess your strengths and weaknesses with respect to these elements. You will then learn how to incorporate these elements into your thinking and actions and maintain an optimal mindset for emotional wellness and lasting happiness.

Please resist any thoughts you might have about how hard or how difficult it will be to complete this learning successfully. In my experience, living one's whole life without this learning is a lot harder! Your efforts to discover more enduring peace and happiness by learning what is in this book will also be far more productive and certain than pursuing tiring and ultimately fruitless notions that we can somehow extract them from circumstance. The Building Blocks, exercises, and Study Guide Questions have been specifically designed to systematically guide you through this learning process and strengthen your grasp on the specifics of creating more sustainable happiness and handling life's circumstances on your own.

The guide will also instruct you on how you can best maintain these improvements in well-being over time. Towards the end of the book, you will find out about the implications of this material for improving parenting, interpersonal relationships, education and performance in the workplace. If you need further help, the guide provides suggestions for finding it. The last few pages of the book provide references, a short annotated bibliography, some additional instructional materials, and an integral notebook for jotting down information on the exercises as well as personal notes. To make the how-to focus of this book easier and more helpful for readers, there are summaries of the key discussion points along with practical Study Guide Questions at the end of every chapter.

Very Important: Please make certain you complete the exercises and answer the Study Guide Questions as you read each Building Block before moving ahead so you receive the full benefit from this book.

Now, before starting Building Block 1, please turn to page 210 at the back of this book entitled, "Reader Progress Evaluation and Feedback Form." On the upper section, under Part 1, you will see instructions for rating yourself on four important questions. Please complete the ratings under "My Level Before Reading This Book" now. You will be given a chance to rate yourself again on these questions after you have completed the book. By comparing the before-and-after ratings, you will be able to gauge the benefits of your learning. (Note: The "% safe versus % unsafe thinking" question in the "rectangular box" should be answered after you read Building Block 2, and again when you have finished the book.)

1

Building Block 1: Mary and Jane and the Roller Coaster Ride

Things don't cause feelings; your thinking about Things does.

Understanding your feelings and emotions and how to self-regulate them is essential for optimal happiness. Whether you feel happy and well-adjusted or struggle with unhappiness and emotional disturbance largely depends upon how well you understand and manage your emotions. Do you understand what makes you feel happy or sad? Do you know what causes your feelings or where they come from? Your mental health and happiness may very well depend upon having the correct answer to these questions. By reading this first Building Block, you will have a clearer understanding about the causes of your emotions.

To get a better perspective on this issue, let's begin by meeting Mary and Jane at a roller coaster. Imagine standing in line in front of a tall, twisting roller coaster ride. Immediately ahead of us are two women. As you may have already guessed, they are Mary and Jane. Mary and Jane are now approaching the very front of the line and they appear to be having a discussion about whether or not they still agree to go on the ride. As we listen in, we hear Mary saying to Jane:

"Come on Jane, we already waited at least an hour; won't you go on with me? I'll even pay for your ticket. You know this ride is really exciting; everyone says it's a lot of fun."

"Well Mary," Jane replies, "the closer we get to this ride, the worse I feel about going on it. It's really starting to frighten me; look how high it is! I'm afraid it's going to make me sick."

As I listen in on what they are saying, something doesn't make sense to me. I feel compelled to enter into their conversation.

"Excuse me, but I happened to overhear your conversation and I just couldn't help being puzzled about it."

Mary replies, "Well just what is it you want to know?"

"Well Mary," I ask, "please explain what's going on between you two."

"I'm glad you asked," Mary says, "I told my friend Jane that I would really like her to go on the ride with me; after all, we waited in line all this time. I even told her I would pay for her ticket, and she turned me down flat."

"Well," I reply, "I'm sorry to hear that." Then I turn to Jane and ask, "What is your take on this, Jane?"

Jane answers, "Some friend! I told Mary this ride is really starting to scare me; it's going to make me sick. At this point, I don't think there is any way I could go on that thing."

Still feeling confused by their explanations, I decide to press on, telling them that I'm still not very clear about something.

Mary says, "What else do you need to know now?"

"Well Mary, I guess I would like to know just how this roller coaster ride makes you feel like it's the best thing since sliced bread, and at the very same time, makes Jane feel awful. Just how is *it* doing that? How is a roller coaster—a big, inanimate contraption of wood and steel—simultaneously causing one of you to feel so excited, and the other completely terrified?" I am tempted to say, "Does it have little wires going into your head, Mary, making you feel excited, and other wires, going into your head, Jane, making you feel afraid?" I decide not to push my luck.

At this point, Mary tires of my questions and tells me that she doesn't want to pursue these "philosophical discussions" any further. She begins to walk away saying, "If you will pardon us, my friend and I are going to leave now, and I'm afraid you will just have to answer your own pesky questions." And so we are left standing in line with my questions still unanswered.

Well, maybe it's understandable that Mary and Jane decided not to answer any more of my questions; after all, I was being a little intrusive. However, my unresolved dilemma is that both women seemed to be attributing their differing feelings to the same physical source: an inanimate roller coaster. How is that possible? How could this amusement ride—this contraption of wood and steel—cause completely opposite emotions in these

3

women? In fairness to them, maybe they thought, "It's just a roller coaster ride," and "why in the world should we have to explain why we feel the way we do?"

Whether they could see it or not, my conversation with Mary and Jane leads into a discussion of greater importance than roller coasters and how we feel about them. The roller coaster metaphor opens up the larger issue of how we actually perceive the causes of our emotions, and the ups and downs in our lives. In light of this metaphor, Mary and Jane may be able to walk away from the roller coaster ride, dismissing my probing questions about what is making them like or dislike the ride. However, when it comes to the larger issue of correctly understanding how emotions work and how to best manage our emotional lives, dismissing these questions has serious implications for how well we feel and how well we manage our emotions.

We are commonly embedded in cultural perspectives that foster misunderstanding about how our emotions work. For some examples, reflect upon these commonly used phrases:

"You hurt my feelings."

"She really embarrassed me."

"That makes me angry."

"He turns me off."

"She turns me on."

"That amusement ride scares me."

All of these statements externalize the causes of our emotions. But as you can see in the roller coaster story, these feelings are really the product of our thinking; they are rooted in the ways we have learned to perceive things, not the world around us. Although these phrases may sound familiar—they may even be phrases we ourselves have used on occasion—none of them are factually correct. However, when we are schooled in emotional misunderstandings through dialogues heard in the family and common culture, we can readily begin to act like the people and Things in the world around us are the cause of our emotions, rather than our own thinking.

Because we live in a world where people often behave as though the world around them is responsible for how they feel, many of us mistakenly learn to think that external events (people, the weather, the stock market, etc.) cause us to feel the way we do. Fortunately, the simple truth is that they don't. Although we may have learned to think otherwise, no roller coaster, mishap, fortune, compliment, or insult makes us feel the way we do. When you begin to hear yourself say, "It makes me feel," stop and ask yourself, "Who is *it*, and how does *it* do that?" Remember this answer: "It" is you!

The key point here is this: with the exception of certain physical experiences like encountering boiling oil, *Things* generally do not make you feel as you do. Instead, it is your *thinking* about Things that does. Think sadly and you will feel sad. Think calmly and you will feel calm. Think angrily and you will feel angry. Think pleasingly and you will feel pleased. When it comes to emotions, what you think is what you get, period. When we attribute our feelings to Things or situations outside of ourselves, we become snared in "situation-bound" thinking. By situation-bound, I mean that when these situations occur, we incorrectly believe the situation causes us to feel the way we do; we respond to the situation in a reflexive, externally determined way. Whenever the "upsetting Thing" occurs, we become upset about it.

Whenever we fail to see that our emotions are first and foremost a product of our own thinking, we act like the environment is controlling us, and behave in a situation-bound fashion. For example, a man who thinks, "cloudy days are depressing" will feel down whenever it's cloudy. He mistakenly attributes his feelings to the conditions of the weather. Because of this incorrect cause and effect thinking, he behaves as though the weather is causing his mood, rather than his thinking about the weather. Since he can't change the weather, and since he thinks the weather is causing his feelings, he is stuck feeling this way; he is situation-bound. He will just have to feel down until the weather improves. Whenever we become situation-bound, we give up personal power and opportunity to gain optimal regulation over our emotions and our lives.

Let's make sure you really understand that thoughts, not Things or situations, govern feelings. Imagine that today is Caitlin's wedding day. Her dress is magnificent, she looks beautiful, the day is picture-perfect, and all of her many friends and family are there for the special occasion. If we judge how she is feeling from the situation, we might too easily conclude that she is ecstatic. We will be wrong in this instance. At this moment, Caitlin is thinking about a former man in her life. She wonders if she is making the right decision, and, despite the outward appearances of the situation, she is not happy. At this moment, she is quite troubled.

Ted has just lost his job. He has three young children at home, a big mortgage on his house, and his mother has recently suffered a stroke. The situation may look bad. Although Ted is concerned, he isn't that down about it. He realizes he has lived through other challenges. He reminds himself that facing his challenges is far better than worrying about them. He accepts that giving his best is all he can do to move forward. The situation hasn't defined how Ted feels; Ted has defined how he feels about the situation.

Recognizing the influence of our thinking on our emotions, leading proponents of Cognitive Behavioral Therapy, such as Albert Ellis (1998, 2006), have developed highly effective techniques for helping people to curb their self-disturbing thinking and manage their emotions more effectively. Using his ABC model, Ellis depicts the relationship between thinking and emotions in the following way: there is an activating event (A) which triggers a thought or belief (B) about the event which, in turn, causes a feeling or emotional consequence (C). A central notion throughout his work, and my own, is that our disturbed feelings are more often the result of incorrect thinking than an external stimulus or situation. This key explanation about how our emotions work is illustrated below:

Emotional Causation

Correct View

STIMULUS (ROLLER COASTER) → THOUGHT CHOICES: SCARY,

EXCITING.

→ EMOTION OPTIONS: FEAR, EXCITEMENT

Incorrect View

STIMULUS (ROLLER COASTER → SITUATION-BOUND-THINKING: "IT

WILL SCARE ME"

→ EMOTION: AFFRAID

To summarize, you now know that your emotions come from your thoughts. While you may occasionally have limited control over external events, you do have the ability to decide what you think. By changing your thinking, you can directly influence how you feel. Knowing that you can have this influence on your thinking is the first step in understanding how to create more lasting joy and contentment in your life.

As you end this first chapter, it is very important that you really notice and remember what I am about to say. Many people want quick solutions to their problems. They would like to have the answers after reading a chapter or two. Don't be one of them! The building blocks have been named as such for a reason: The first seven lay a foundation, then the next three (Building Blocks 8, 9, and 10) get to the heart of the matter with the answers. Have faith; the benefits of this book are within your reach, just a

few chapters away. However, the right way to achieve them is to proceed through each chapter in sequence so that you have the necessary learning foundation. This way is the way to get what you came for!

Some Points to Remember

Many of us think that circumstances around us cause our feelings and emotions. When we think this way, we become situation-bound and lose a lot of control over our feelings and our happiness. Fortunately for us, it is really our thinking about these Things that causes our emotions, not the circumstances surrounding us. Realizing that your thinking causes your emotions, and recognizing that you always have the option to change how you look at your life, gives you the opportunity to change and improve how you feel. Think right and you will feel right.

Study Guide Questions

1. In the roller coaster ride story, Jane explains to Mary why she doesn't want to go on the ride by saying, "I'm afraid it's going to make me sick." How might Jane have expressed her reluctance to go on the ride without making "it" the cause of her feelings?

2. If the roller coaster isn't the primary cause of Mary's excitement, what is?

3. According to the ABC model of Albert Ellis, Mary's emotion of excitement would be an example of A, B, or C?

4. Correct the following statement, "That really bothers me."

5. Think of two examples in your own thinking where you have incorrectly assigned the cause of your feelings to Things rather than to your own thinking.

6. Write down what you consider to be the most important idea from having read this building block.

2

Building Block 2: Safe and Unsafe Thinking

To feel well, you must first think well

If your feelings derive from your thoughts, what is it about your thinking that causes you to feel different emotions? In this section, you will learn about the types of thinking that produce your positive and negative feelings and emotions. Before exploring these thought patterns, I would like to describe a circumstance that prompted the development of this Building Block.

About 25 years ago I was working with a middle-aged woman one evening when the notion of safe and unsafe thinking first occurred to me. She was talking about her problems, one after the other, and becoming more and more upset. As I thought about her behavior, I began to think of her thought patterns as the emotional equivalent of someone driving down the wrong side of the road—it was emotionally hazardous and unsafe —unsafe thinking! Under any circumstance, this style of thinking is bound to upset anyone. Pursuing this line of reasoning further, I thought to myself, "there are, or there ought to be, some 'rules of the highway' that help us keep this kind of thinking in check so we don't get ourselves so disturbed." I wondered if there were ways of thinking that would not only help prevent states of emotional disturbance, but would also help improve states of emotional health and happiness. Might this notion of safe and unsafe thinking be a key factor in both the creation and loss of emotional well-being? Most importantly, if there were right and wrong ways of thinking on our thinking and feeling highway, are we able to learn what the rules are so we can manage emotional stress and disturbance more effectively? Can we follow these guidelines to generate more enduring happiness? These were intriguing questions to me, so I began to pursue them.

Over the years, I continued to explore these interests in my private practice. I want to share what I have found with you because the knowledge I gained has proven to be very useful in helping others learn how to better manage their feelings and emotions and live happier lives. As we go into the details, I first want you to be clear about what I mean when I use the terms safe and unsafe thinking. By safe thinking I am referring to any type of thought that produces a positive feeling or emotion. Examples of this type of thinking would be thoughts such as, "I feel really good about who I am," or "I love being out in nature." Unsafe thinking is thinking that gives rise to a negative feeling or emotion. "Why am I such a loser?" is an example of unsafe thinking. Another example would be, "I hate flying." Note that any person who seriously thinks these types of thoughts is guaranteed to feel bad—there is no escaping it. No matter what, we will always make ourselves feel bad whenever we think these thoughts. In brief, safe thinking creates positive feelings that enhance our well-being; unsafe thinking disturbs us and diminishes our well-being.

Before going any further, I want to make it clear that I am not suggesting we should never have unsafe thoughts, or that all unsafe thinking is bad or unwarranted. Although prolonged unsafe thinking is generally bad for emotional and physical well-being, it is only natural that all of us will have these thoughts at times. We all encounter emotionally challenging situations from time to time, such as the death of a loved one, job loss, rejection, or other setbacks. During hard times, troubling emotions like grief, remorse, sadness, or anger are certainly human and understandable, given the gravity of the challenges confronting our sense of well-being.

Still, we need to remain ever mindful of our unsafe thinking because it always places a burden on our well-being.[4] Keep in mind that prolonged unsafe thinking generally does very little to remedy or change a problem. It actually tends to perpetuate it. On the other hand, since safe thinking produces states of positive feeling that we associate with happiness, sustaining this kind of thinking directly improves our emotional well-being. In the next Building Block, entitled "Emotions as a Signal System," you will learn more about how you can best use

---

[4] Some individuals are prone to over-employ negative thinking to anticipate what can go wrong and plan more effective actions; or to motivate and sanction behavior. Although it is important to understand the implications of our actions and head off wrongful consequences, there are usually better ways to accomplish these objectives that preserve well-being and minimize emotional disturbance.

the emotional signals generated from your safe and unsafe thinking as guides in promoting and regulating emotional health and happiness.

Recognizing the particular types of thinking that cause our positive and negative feelings is not very hard to do but people sometimes have difficulty with this concept in the beginning. I think that part of this difficulty stems from our tendency to look at our feelings and our thoughts as two separate things. We may not fully recognize that certain types of thoughts actually create the positive and negative feelings we have. In particular, thoughts that stir us and convey significant meanings to us frequently create strong feelings. Understandably, the idea that our thinking is the force causing our emotions often seems a little strange to us at first.

Let's work a little more on identifying the types of thinking that shape your emotions, starting with the kind of thinking that would cause you to experience negative feelings or emotions. I want you to begin with this unsafe thinking first because most people find it easier to identify examples of unsafe (negative) thinking than examples of safe (or positive) thinking. Perhaps because we are conditioned or genetically engineered to be more focused on the problems and troubles in our world than the nice stuff, we can recognize our patterns of negative thinking more readily. People will say, "For some reason, it seems to be a lot harder to think of the types of thoughts that make a person feel good than the ones that make them feel bad." If this is the case, small wonder well-being and happiness can be so elusive.

By type of unsafe thinking, I am referring to a category of thought that will cause you to feel a particular unpleasant emotion, for example, fear. See if you can identify a type of unsafe thinking that would cause you, or anyone else for that matter, to feel really upset. Remember, your emotions are not fixed reactions to external circumstances; they are caused by your thinking and your beliefs. Your thinking and emotions are not separate things; they are tightly interconnected. What is a type of thinking that will cause you to have negative emotions? Think of an example.

There is always a connection between these types of thinking and your feelings. Recall for example, "think angrily and you will feel angry." Angry thinking is one common type of unsafe thinking. It is almost so obvious that you could easily miss seeing it. So, if you were to make yourself feel angry about a man who just took the parking spot you were planning to pull into by thinking angry thoughts like, "What a jerk, the nerve of this guy," the type of unsafe thinking you would be engaging in is anger thinking. You would be thinking thoughts that generate the sentiments of anger.

Worry represents another type of unsafe thinking. After meeting her potential Mr. Right, Megan immediately begins to doubt whether he will ever call her back. As she engages in this type of thinking, she begins to feel worried. She is engaging in a type of unsafe thinking that makes her feel worried and uneasy. Her specific unsafe thoughts may be something like, "Will he call me? I am afraid he might never call me back." This type of

15

unsafe thinking causes the disturbing feeling of worry and may have Megan sitting around waiting for the phone to ring. This thinking is unsafe thinking because when Megan thinks this way, she makes herself worried and anxious and causes her emotional well-being to diminish.

For each negative emotion such as fear, anger, grief, sadness and so on, there is a type of unsafe thinking that causes it. This thinking helps form the nature and intensity of our emotional experience. One way to identify the type of unsafe thinking that causes you to feel a certain emotion is to focus first on the kind of emotional feeling you experience, guilt for example. Once you have identified this emotion as one of guilt, you can more readily get in touch with the specific guilty thinking that is causing you to have these feelings. For example, I notice that I feel guilty about something and eventually discover that I am thinking, "Mom seemed tired, I should have helped her out more with cleaning up at the party." This is why I am feeling guilty.

Note that anger, fear, and many negative emotions cause our body to release adrenalin and other neurotransmitters. In turn, these chemicals cause certain physiological reactions like rapid breathing, increased heart rate and sensations of physiological arousal. These physical responses also become associated with various emotional "feelings." I suspect most of us are more likely to recall the situation that we got upset about, or the physiological reactions we experienced, than the actual thoughts which first triggered our feelings. With a little practice you will be able to ferret out most of the thinking that causes your feelings. You now have a much better chance of correctly regulating how you feel because you have correctly identified the cause of your feelings.

In the table below, I list some of the most common types of unsafe thinking people have and the negative emotions these types of thoughts generate. We may interpret these disturbing emotions as the result of bad luck or circumstance. We may also believe that we must feel badly when certain situations occur, but if we follow such faulty reasoning, we will be especially vulnerable to making ourselves feel bad whenever we encounter these situations. For better or worse, our feelings and emotions are not the product of circumstance; they are the product of what we learned to think. Most importantly, you can greatly improve how you feel by improving how you think about various situations. Take time now to carefully examine the list of unsafe thinking presented below. Notice how every type of disturbing feeling and emotion on this list results from a specific type of unsafe thinking. Our thoughts—various types of unsafe thinking —cause different negative feelings.

Unsafe Thinking List

Type of Unsafe Thinking	Feeling
Angry thoughts—"How dare he insult me like this?"	Anger
Sad thoughts—"I miss her terribly"	Sad
Resentful thoughts—"You're making me do all the work"	Resentful
Self-blaming thoughts—"I never do anything right"	Unworthy

Hurt thoughts—"Alex never even called on my birthday"   Hurt

Unpleasant thoughts—"Another gloomy day"   Unpleasant

Worrisome thoughts—"What if I need another operation?"   Worried

Fearful thoughts—"That roller coaster is scary"   Afraid

Anxious thoughts—"What if we can't find our way back?"   Anxious

Boring thoughts—"It's always the same old thing"   Bored

Overwhelmed thoughts—"I can't handle one more thing"   Overwhelmed

Pressure thoughts—"I must get this done right away"   Pressured

Grief thoughts—"I can't imagine living without her"   Grief

Annoyed thoughts—"Stop playing with the remote"   Annoyed

Please take time now to identify three types of unsafe thinking that you engage in from time to time. For each of these, write down the specific unsafe thinking and the emotion or feeling caused by this thinking.

Example 1.

Example 2.

Example 3.

Can you think of any other types of unsafe thinking that you would put on this list?

Not only are all of these different negative emotions the product of unsafe thinking, but the intensity of these emotions is also a product of our thinking. We create the intensity by the degree of meaning and importance we attach to these thoughts. The worse (more catastrophic, worrisome, terrible, etc.) we believe something is, the more intense the negative emotion will be. If you strongly endorse the idea that going to the dentist will be terrible, you will certainly make yourself feel awful about your upcoming dental appointment. By realizing that you cause the intensity of your negative emotions, you can learn to control them better by altering the content of your unsafe thinking. Successfully altering your unsafe thinking will make your emotions less intense. For example, instead of thinking, "I really hate public speaking," you might choose to think, "Public speaking is a challenge, but I'm working on getting better at it." You can also deepen positive emotions by enriching and intensifying safe thinking.

Pay closer attention to the types of unsafe thinking you have when you feel upset. Keep track of this information in a journal or in the space for notes provided at the back of this book so you can begin changing your thinking. Notice which types of unsafe thinking you have and how often you have them. In Building Block Seven, you will find a number of techniques you can use to reduce unsafe thinking and improve control over your emotions.

Mastering unsafe thinking is an important component of achieving emotional well-being, but it is not the whole story. Avoiding negative thoughts is not the same thing as knowing how to sustain a positive, emotionally healthy existence. To feel well and experience more enduring happiness, there are other emotional skills we must possess. Knowing how to think safely is one of them.

The crux of maintaining happiness and emotional well-being rests with our ability to create, sustain, and increase our positive emotions over time. We promote these goals through safe thinking. We can only feel well if we are thinking well. Therefore, understanding how safe thinking works and how to use it regularly is especially important for maintaining your happiness. Resting your emotional happiness upon a scoreboard tally of your "doings and strivings" will not bring about sustainable happiness. Attaching your emotional welfare to this scoreboard will lead you right into situation-bound, up and down thinking, and eliminate any possibility of sustaining happiness and emotional well-being, unless you always win. Relying upon drugs—prescribed or otherwise—won't do it either; none of these alternatives do anything to correct or improve the emotional knowledge we all must have to stay emotionally happy and well.

To have the kind of peace and joy that you can really maintain, you need to internalize a proper foundation. This core foundation comes about from emotional learning, learning that generates safe thinking and offers you the ability to stabilize and sustain your well-being despite inevitable fluctuations in life circumstances. You won't always be able to control life circumstances, however, with this learning you will be better equipped to deal with them. You will know how to maintain happiness as the world around you continues to have its ups and downs. With this knowledge, old alternatives like fretting and worrying whenever Things aren't going well will be seen as the colossal and self-defeating wastes of time that they are. Similarly, you will no longer wait for Things to be right in order to be happy; instead, this knowledge will give you the initiative and power to experience happiness on your own terms. You will be happy while you are waiting for Things to happen.

Now, let's look more closely at the types of safe thinking that generate important feelings of emotional wellness and cause us to be happy. Emotionally speaking, this is the kind of thinking that keeps us on the right side of the road. As I mentioned earlier, many of us are less able to recognize or describe these patterns of thinking. One way to help yourself recognize these patterns is to focus in on the type of thinking you have when you experience a positive emotion. As with unsafe thinking, for any positive emotion you experience, there is also a type of safe thinking that causes you to experience this positive feeling. Your feelings do not come from something outside of you. It is your mind's safe thinking that causes these emotions.

Now, try to come up with an example of safe thinking. Can you think of any other examples? Write down your examples here:

In the table on the next page, I have listed several types of safe thinking and the feelings we experience when we engage in these thoughts. Please take time now to look over this list. Study this list carefully. Notice how each of these positive feelings or emotions results from a particular type of thinking. Again, this is only a partial list of some types of safe thinking. When it comes to safe thinking, the universe is practically unlimited—there are thousands upon thousands of these thoughts.

After you have examined this list, practice remembering the categories of safe thinking. Ask yourself if safe thinking happens when you choose it to, or if it usually only happens when you encounter certain situations, which trigger these thoughts. How often do you engage in safe thinking? Are you able to elicit these thoughts when you wish to? If you are not accustomed to engaging in safe thinking on a regular basis, **or** if you usually think this way only when situations prompt you to, you should start working on increasing safe thinking now.

Building Block 7 has some great tips for how you can approach this. Your goal should be to engage safe thinking throughout every day. Pay particular attention to how thinking positively elevates your mood. Noticing this benefit not only reinforces the habit of safe thinking, it is one of the essential steps in raising your overall level of personal happiness and well-being.

Safe Thinking List

Type of Safe Thinking	Feeling
Joyous Thoughts—"Our baby is healthy and beautiful"	Joyful
Fun thoughts—"I love skiing"	Excited or happy
Funny thoughts—"That's hilarious"	Like laughing
Calming thoughts—"Everything will be OK"	Peaceful
Pleasant thoughts—"What a beautiful day"	Pleasant
Reassuring thoughts—"I am good at my work"	Confident
Forgiving thoughts—"We all make mistakes"	Forgiven/ Forgiving
Patient thoughts—"I just need more practice"	Less tense
Favorite things—"My cat is too cute for words"	Happy/pleased
Contented thoughts—"I could not ask for more"	Contentment
Looking forward thoughts—"I can't wait to see him"	Excited
Successful thoughts—"We played so well this season"	Proud
Grateful thoughts—"We have a good life"	Grateful
Relieving thoughts—"This too shall pass"	Relieved
Loving thoughts—"I cherish her"	Love

Accepting thoughts—"I like who I am"	Acceptance
Awesome thoughts—"The light in that painting is amazing"	Awe
'Things are great' thoughts—"I am loving this vacation"	Terrific

Before concluding this section, I would like to make a couple of additional comments on the subject of positive thinking. If we lacked the ability to think positively, we would be condemned to a life where emotional well-being, happiness, and mental health were impossible. I am aware that some people view positive thinking with skepticism. They regard it as merely painting over reality with false optimism, or a strategy of excessive denial. But such skepticism too quickly portrays positive thinking as wrong—that it is gratuitous and unrealistic to be so happy in such an imperfect world. The skeptics seem to be telling us, "If things are bad, it's only right and realistic to feel bad." To me, this sounds more like a rationale for being unhappy and not a very logical one at that.

You do not necessarily have to feel bad about bad Things just because they exist. In fact, doing so only guarantees that you will make yourself feel bad. Moreover, feeling bad about Things never changes them. For the most part, feeling bad just strips away your joy and lowers your resilience for coping. So, some of the very best things you can do are think positively and engage in safe thoughts. Thinking positively actually helps you to cope better with some of these problems.

You shouldn't deny that problems exist; you just shouldn't let yourself get caught up in negative thinking about them. Instead, work on dealing with problems the best way you can. Choose to faithfully retain, rather than dispose of, your happiness in the face of life's problems.

Some Points to Remember

Some types of thinking cause negative emotions. Unsafe types, like angry thinking, sad thinking, fearful thinking and worry thinking cause you to feel disturbed and upset. Safe types of thinking, like grateful thinking, joyous thinking, peaceful thinking, and acceptance thinking, promote feeling well and happy. Whether you feel disturbed or well is more a matter of choice than circumstance, so you don't necessarily have to feel bad when Things go bad. Help yourself to feel and stay well longer by choosing safe thinking over unsafe thinking. Safe thinking will work much better for you.

Study Guide Questions

1. In general, when you engage in unsafe thinking, you will feel _____?

2. Why is safe thinking generally better for your emotional well-being?

3. Identify three broad *types* of unsafe thinking.

4. Give a specific example of the thinking for each of these types of unsafe thinking.

5. Think of two occasions when you got yourself very upset about something. What unsafe thinking triggered these feelings?

6. List three broad *types* of safe thinking.

7. Think about how much time you now spend in safe and unsafe thinking throughout the day. Estimate these percentages. Now set a target goal for raising the percentage of safe thinking and lowering the amount of unsafe thinking you do. Write down these numbers here (also enter the percentages for "now" on the Reader Progress Evaluation and Feedback Form on

page 210):

NOW		GOAL	
% SAFE ( )	% UNSAFE ( )	% SAFE ( )	% UNSAFE ( )

8. Make a list of unsafe thinking that you wish to change.

3

Building Block 3: Emotions as a Signal System For Well-being

Negative emotions are not states to stay in; they are signals for action

All humans have the ability to experience a wide range of feelings or emotions. Our emotions give us the ability to react to danger as well as to experience important meaning in life—to savor our triumphs and rue our misfortunes. We have these feelings, but why do we have them? What purpose do they serve? In this section, you will have the opportunity to deepen your knowledge of how your emotions work and how to regulate them. You will learn how to view your emotions as a bio-psychological *signal system* and find out how you can best use this signal system to promote better mental health and well-being. You will also learn how safe and unsafe thinking play key roles in this process. The material presented here will increase your understanding and ability to regulate how you feel, improve your mood, and promote sustained happiness.

We know that one purpose our emotions serve is to assist us with self-protection, for example, our fight-or-flight response.

From an evolutionary perspective, it is reasonable to assume that we developed responses like anger and fear because these emotions helped us cope with threats to our survival. We walk upright, talk and have the ability to process complex information because being able to do so enabled us to stay alive, compete amongst ourselves and other organisms. With this reasoning, we developed our capacities for emotions like anger and fear because they helped us with our survival needs. These emotions are there to help us fight or flee. Experiencing emotions like fear and anger enables us to respond more effectively and protectively when we are confronted by threats to our welfare. Our emotions not only alert us to impending threats, they also ramp up our body's physical preparedness (heart rate, breathing, blood volume, musculature, pupil dilation, etc.), helping us avoid or ward off threats. We may have even used the energizing properties of these emotions to ward off saber tooth tigers and other predators or to get the heck away from them as fast as possible—pretty important stuff in the history of human survival.

But we should also note that living in a safer world has clearly lessened our day-to-day need for our more primitive protective reactions. Hopefully, many of us will rarely encounter a real threat to our physical safety. Living in a friendlier world is far different from our primitive past, when the emotional fight-or-flight system was routinely needed for day-to-day survival. Assuming we are not in police work, or octagon fighters, how often do we really need to fire up these protective emotions of fear and anger in our daily lives? How often do we actually encounter the kinds of serious physical threats or situations where anger or fear-based flight is the best response?

Although times have most certainly changed for many of us, our bodies continue to have the fight-or-flight response at the ready. In today's world, however, these protective emotions often get in the way. Too often these emotions get activated at the wrong time and for the wrong reasons, sometimes creating more harm than good. Road rage is but one unfortunate example. Resulting from poorly controlled anger, road rage can have very serious consequences in our increasingly litigious society. Emotional volatility and aggression on the road, at home, in school, or in the workplace continue to be sources of serious social concern. Unchecked, our fight-or-flight emotions have damaging consequences for our social relationships and for our emotional and physical health. These emotions can worsen cardiovascular disease as well as other physical ailments. Moreover, protracted periods of fear, worry, or anger can help bring about a variety of emotional maladies including anxiety disorders, depression, stress, exhaustion, as well as many other psychological problems. Given the seriousness of these concerns, we owe it to ourselves to become more proficient in understanding and managing our emotional behavior. Our mental health, social welfare, happiness and well-being all depend upon it.

We also possess many emotions besides fear and anger. Some of these emotions occur when we experience ecstasy, feel happy and peaceful, stimulate states of worry and sadness, or start reasoning a life of existential dread. Why do we have all these other emotions and feelings? Is there an overarching explanation for why we experience this diversity of good and bad feelings, an explanation that would offer us a deeper understanding of their purpose and how we can best utilize them?

I believe that a more complete explanation emerges when we start looking at our emotions as energizing signals that are there to support both our physical safety and our emotional well-being. All of our emotions (pleasant and unpleasant) can be viewed as signals; they are important feedback signals meant to preserve and enhance our physical and psychological well-being, and to ward off potential threats. When we experience a negative feeling (like fear or anxiety) or a positive one (like joy or peacefulness), we receive one of these important, energizing signals. These signals convey information to us about whether something seems good or bad. These signals come from your thoughts. When you feel sad or down, for example, the emotional signal your thoughts send is that something is not right. When you feel happy, the signal generated through your thinking is that Things are looking good or even great. Your emotions function as an ongoing signal system providing you with important psychological feedback that is vital to the proper regulation of your physical and emotional health. By tuning in to these signals and learning how to use your emotional signal system as it is designed to work, you can become more proficient in regulating your emotions, guiding your behavior, and enhancing your emotional well-being.

Now let's zoom in on the connection between these emotional signals and our safe and unsafe thinking. Unsafe thinking is your brain's way of alerting you through worry, sadness, grief or some other emotional signal that something appears to be wrong, that you perceive a problem. It is important to realize that as long as you think this way, you will continue to experience the disturbing emotion of fear, anger, or worry, etc. The disturbing emotion will not go away until the unsafe thinking goes away—until you change this thinking.

How should you respond to your signals of emotional disturbance? The main purpose of these signals is to stimulate actions that serve to resolve or remove the disturbance. You need to take a corrective action to restore a positive state of mind when these signals appear. In responding to these signals of disturbance, you must first determine whether the unsafe thinking behind the emotional signal is really justified. You need to be certain that this warning signal warrants your reaction to it. Explore your options. Is it best for you to try to change the situation, or should you simply try changing your thinking about it? Check the accuracy of your thinking. The signal (fear for example) might be based on a valid perception of endangerment requiring action on your part. On the other hand, this signal might just be the result of a misperception or overreaction in your thinking. If so, there may be little or no benefit in taking action to this signal other than that of calming yourself down by thinking differently.

Suppose the emotional signal is one that prompts anger over who has rights to a parking spot. An unchecked response to this anger could lead to a shouting match, or worse yet, a physical confrontation. Overreacting to these emotional false alarms is unwise and possibly dangerous. In this instance, the correct response would be to turn off the unsafe anger thinking that is erroneously signaling a serious violation to our welfare and prompting the urge to leap into a confrontation.

When we experience emotions that signal a problem, we do need to take action to reduce the disturbance. The question is, which action? We need to be mindful about taking the proper action. In the missed parking spot example, we are better served by "shutting off" the anger thoughts, than by letting them propel us into an angry confrontation. There is no real physical threat and an angry confrontation will only make matters worse, not better. On the other hand, if you realize that a store clerk grossly overcharged you and you are feeling upset about it, reacting to this signal by discussing this problem with the store clerk or the store manager could result in a benefit to your well-being. Getting upset over this circumstance, while doing nothing about it, will not.

So, when unsafe thinking disturbs us, we need to make a decision that will turn off the emotional warning light and resolve these feelings. Choose to take action in response to the unsafe thinking if there is a valid basis for action, or turn this thinking off, if there is not. You do not want to let yourself get caught in the middle where you continue to stay in a state of disturbance and do neither of these things. When your unsafe thinking prompts you to feel these alarm signals of emotional unease, your job is always to take corrective action—by thought or by deed—to resolve the disturbance. This is in keeping with both the adaptive purpose and optimal use of your emotional signal system.

Realize that emotional difficulties and disorders like anxiety and depression and so many others most often result from staying in states of unsafe thinking. When you do this, rather than take actions that will improve circumstances or your thoughts about them, you invite emotional trouble. You are then allowing yourself to ignore, or improperly act with respect to your emotional signal system, and you jeopardize your emotional well-being. Be mindful about staying on the right side of the emotional road and promptly heeding these signals of disturbance.

To maintain the state of feeling well, make sure you avoid getting stuck in the middle of your unsafe thinking where you continue to disturb yourself about something, while doing nothing about it. All that this will accomplish for you is to make you feel bad. If, for example, you were to continue to harbor angry thoughts about a man who took "your" parking space well after the time when this event occurred, you would be falling into this emotional trap. Regrets and resentments all stem from this kind of faulty thinking. Perpetuating unsafe thinking only serves to make you feel needlessly disturbed, longer. Do you know anyone in your life that makes a habit out of dwelling on the negative events way too much, draining both your energy and theirs? Think of the emotional alarms sounded by your unsafe thinking signals as signals for action, not states to stay in. Use them or lose them, but don't keep them turned on.

The chief purpose of unsafe thinking is to signal you, by way of a disturbed feeling, that something appears to be wrong and, to energize coping action, if needed, to resolve it. To manage this part of our emotional signal system well, we simply need to act in ways that reduce the disturbance rationally, and in a timely manner. This seems reasonable enough and adaptive, but what about your safe emotional thinking?

What is the function—the adaptive purpose—of the safe thoughts that produce your positive feelings and emotions? Safe thoughts certainly make us feel good and contribute to our happiness, but are they also energizing signals? If they are, for what? Indeed, they are energizing signals, and they do have a very important purpose. Whenever you experience some kind of positive emotion, you have a safe emotional thought, a confirmation that something feels good for your well-being, that something seems right. For example, when you experience laughter or delight, you receive these positive emotional signals.

What information are the signals that arise from your safe thinking conveying to you, and what is their energizing purpose? Assuming that a properly calibrated moral and rational compass informs your thinking, these signals are indicating that you are interpreting things favorably. Your thoughts are giving you positive feedback that is making you feel good in this moment. By way of these positive emotional signals, you can detect that you are engaging in some type of safe thinking that is favorable to your well-being. The experience you are having is reinforcing to your well-being. Repeating and building upon favorable thoughts and actions that generate these positive signals improves your mood and well-being. Safe thinking helps you to feel well and appears to enhance other behavior that engenders well-being.[5]

You can think relaxing thoughts to feel more relaxed or engage in actions that prompt thoughts and feelings of relaxation. By way of example, you could muse about a relaxing day at the beach or go spend a day at the beach, to prompt the thinking, which gives you the pleasurable feeling state of relaxation. However you should probably decide against repeating excessive alcohol consumption if that is how you have approached acquiring feelings of relaxation. When hard work is necessary, you can wisely avoid feeling poorly about it by prompting thoughts of encouragement and approval to maintain optimism while you get your work done.

By way of our safe thinking, we receive emotional signals telling us that we are thinking and behaving in ways that aide well-being. We sense through these signals that our thoughts or

---

[5] Feeling good just to feel good is not all this is about. Fredrickson (2001) proposes in her "broaden and build" theory that positive emotions like joy and contentment may also serve a deeper evolutionary purpose. She and her colleagues have done research showing that positive emotions build resources that not only make us happier, but also help us to stay healthier and to function in more adaptive ways.

the actions are good for us—these are beneficial signals that energize our coping resources, increase resilience, and enrich our happiness and life satisfaction. For well-being sake, it is good for us to remember how to engage and repeat engaging in these safe thoughts and actions again, and again.

Some Points to Remember

Your safe and unsafe thinking provides you with red light and green light emotional signals that are vital to your state of mind. Paying closer attention to these signals, to how you are feeling in the moment, allows you to take full advantage of this very important emotional feedback system and to improve self-regulation of your emotions and happiness. By listening to these signals carefully, and by adjusting your thoughts and actions to them correctly so that you maximize the signals of wellness and limit the signals of disturbance, you will enhance your ability to adapt and flourish, both physically and emotionally.

Study Guide Questions

1. Your emotions act as a signal system. What are they telling you?

2. When you feel disturbed, what are your best options?

3. What role does unsafe thinking play in this signal system?

4. Why would someone not be using their emotional signal system wisely if he or she continued to stay angry over a situation in their past?

5. When you feel really good about something, what is this emotional signal telling you?

6. Knowing that you have this important emotional signal system, do you see any ways in which you can make this system work better for you?

4

Building Block 4: Little Sara

If it's not good for Little Sara, it's not good for you

You now understand that your emotions work as a complex signal system to promote adaptation. This signal system, when it is working properly, enables you to detect and respond to circumstances that challenge or enhance your well-being. When you use your emotional signal system mindfully and purposefully, you will have better mood regulation and well-being. However, because the emotional signal system is rooted in your thoughts—more specifically in how you have learned to think about Things—how well this system works for you comes down to what you have learned. Did you learn to think safely about most situations most of the time, or did you learn to use too many unsafe thoughts such as worry, anger, sadness, or guilt? What did you learn to think about you? Most importantly, what kind of relationship did you learn to have with yourself?

The key issue is whether or not our life experience taught us how to keep our safe and unsafe thinking in balance and imparted us with the right self-nurturing mindset for optimal emotional functioning and happiness. These are key issues because the quality of our emotional well-being ultimately depends on how well we learned to think emotionally. In this section you will see how life experience shapes the way we sustain or do not sustain happiness, self-nurturance, and emotional well-being. To help all of us understand this topic better, I invented a delightful and loveable little girl named Sara. Little Sara will help you see more clearly how this emotional learning develops. You will see how her emotional experiences affect and shape her emotional learning and emotional health. By seeing what works and doesn't work for Little Sara, you will also get a clearer perspective on the kind of emotional experience and learning we all must cultivate in order to promote a happier life. But before we meet her, I want to talk to you about the client who first prompted me to dream up Little Sara.

About ten years ago, I began working with a man named Len who was in his early 50's. He was generally pleasant but overly stiff, serious, and depressed. As a businessman, Len always wore a suit and tie to our sessions and typically maintained a formal demeanor during our conversations. Except for occasional expressions of anger, he was virtually devoid of other emotions. Len was exceptionally hard on himself, explaining that both he and his sister had a very strict upbringing. At one point, I recall Len saying that he literally couldn't remember what it felt like to have fun.

As he told me about himself, I couldn't help but wonder what it must be like to live inside Len's head: all of the rules, the rush to self-judgment every time he missed his own high water mark, the lack of good humor or personal compassion—all of this

must have made his day-to-day existence very burdensome.
Len's only relief seemed to be buying things like cars, TVs and
gadgets that he didn't really need, or smoking some marijuana or
drinking a few shots of whiskey at the end of the day to relax.

I wondered if Len was even capable of listening to himself;
of really noticing what he felt or noticing what he made himself
feel. If he was capable of listening to himself, did he know what
to do when he felt sad, or hurt, or when his critical internal voice
began chanting, "You're not good enough"? Why was he always
so hard on himself? Why did Len always feel the need to buy
something, smoke something, or drink something to feel better?
Why could he no longer recall what fun feels like? Why had his
emotional signal system and his ability to self-nurture become so
compromised, and most importantly, how do we help this man
move forward?

My mind also reflected on Len's history—his mom was
strict, overly critical, and usually absorbed by other concerns.
Both of his parents were emotionally unavailable to him and his
sister much of the time. How nurturing could this kind of home
life have been for them? It seems that when Len did risk
expressing his emotional needs as a child, his needs usually went
unheard or were overridden by other parental needs and
priorities. Why would a child bother to keep expressing his
feelings or needs—sadness, boredom, disappointment, something
wanted or unwanted—any of them—if his parents often acted as
though they were too busy or didn't care? It is easy to see how
Len learned to shut down emotionally. After all, Len's emotional

signal system was largely ignored. As a child, he must have repeatedly arrived at the conclusion: "It doesn't matter how I feel or how I express my feelings, so why bother feeling anything?"

Under childhood circumstances like these, receiving adequate nurturance and learning about self-tendering goes straight out the window, or at best, becomes a self-taught, hit-or-miss affair. The emotional signal system begins to warp into a learned helplessness, and distress internalizes in the form of anxiety, apathy and depression. Ritualistic efforts at self-soothing and misbehavior often emerge as makeshift substitutes for critical shortages in parental nurturance. Self-soothing stimulation and distraction appear in behaviors like talking to one's self, nervous ticks, excessive nose picking, aberrant masturbation, fighting, negative attention seeking, overeating, under eating—the list can go on and on.

I found myself saying to this man, "Len, do you listen to yourself, do you pay attention to your feelings"? I was hoping this question would prompt him to see how he was ignoring his own feelings, exactly as his parents had done. But, a strange thing happened. Len seemed to have no idea what I was talking about. He kept saying to me, "I don't know what you mean by 'listen to myself'." I tried several more times to explain what I meant, but to no avail. I wanted him to recognize how the way he was treating himself emotionally (more like abandoning himself) was probably the reason why he was angry, depressed, self-deprecating, and otherwise emotionless. Who wouldn't be? How would anyone feel if they habitually ignored their own feelings and mistreated themselves? With Len, there were lots of unsafe thoughts and almost no safe ones—little nurturing from outside, and even less from within. This was a perfect recipe for emotional dysfunction. Len did not know how to listen to his feelings because he had learned early on that his feelings did not really matter much.

Since nurturance is possible only when our feelings listened to, I wanted to teach Len to listen to his feelings so he could nurture himself better. I decided to invent a special person who I hoped might help him listen. I wanted to help him get in touch with the sensing, informing and feeling self we all possess. I would do this by introducing him to an exquisitely sensitive and authentic, example of a feeling self that I began to conjure in my head. I would help Len learn how to listen to his feelings by first having him listen to Little Sara.

Emotionally transparent, loveable and boldly naive, Little Sara would be true to her feelings. She would be someone we would naturally want to nurture and care for, someone innocent and commandingly sincere. She would be absolutely perfect for the part—the embodiment of an emotional litmus test for telling us what feels right for her, and what doesn't. In the most straightforward manner, Little Sara would reveal how all of us are naturally adapted to feel and react when our needs are being met or not met. I hoped Len would better understand what "listening" meant if he began by listening to Little Sara who naturally expresses exactly what she is feeling. All he would have to do is listen to her.

Without knowing exactly how these emerging ideas were going to unfold, I began. "O.K, Len," I said, "to help you see what I mean by 'listening to yourself' I'm going to tell you a story." I described the first scene to him: "I see a very sweet little girl sitting in front of a TV in the morning eating her breakfast. She looks to be only two or so years old. She's watching her favorite show, Barney, (not sure why I picked Barney as this purple dinosaur character was certainly never one of my personal favorites)." As I described the scene, I asked Len to imagine that he was actually there watching everything with me. I asked him to pay very close attention to how the little girl might be feeling as the story progressed. "Listen carefully Len," I said, "try to sense her emotions; try to listen for what she might be feeling."

I described how Little Sara was sitting quietly, enjoying some dry cereal with a cup of orange juice. Eating this breakfast and watching that purple dinosaur on TV were two of her favorite things in the world. Just as she was about to have a few more Cheerios—whoops!—her little foot bumps her cup and orange juice spills onto the living room rug. Now, here comes her mother, rushed and harried. "What's this Sara? Did you spill your juice on the rug? What if it stains? You know I really don't have time for this, Sara. Another mess to clean up; I'm already late for work as it is!"

I asked Len to try sensing what the little girl might be feeling as her mother spoke to her. Continuing with the scene, Little Sara's mom says, "You know Sara, I just spent $85.00 to get this rug cleaned." With the mom's voice growing louder, "You need to be more careful: I really don't have time for this right now. The baby sitter is here, and I have to leave." Looking at my client, I asked him, "What do you notice? Is the little girl's hand shaking a bit? Is her face flushed now? Is that a tear in her eye we see? Are you able to listen to her, to sense what she is most likely feeling?"

Somewhat hesitantly, Len answered, "It seems like she is probably feeling afraid and upset."

With the vivid prompts of this story Len was at least able to listen to Little Sara's feelings. I began to think that we were really starting to get somewhere with the help of Little Sara!

"Good Len, now let's try a different situation," I said, "Scene Two." In this scene, I decided to insert a much kinder and more nurturing person into the mother role, to evoke different feelings in Little Sara. I again asked Len to pay close attention to how the little girl might be feeling as this scene unfolded. In this version of the story Little Sara's mother comes into the room after the orange juice spills, and says to her daughter, "Oh dear, did we have a spill? Don't worry Sara. It's OK. I know you didn't mean to do it. I'll get something to wipe this up." Touching her daughter's arm and wiping the rug, her mother continues, "You know, maybe we need to get you a sippy cup with the special top that won't spill so easily, or perhaps we will have you finish your juice at the kitchen table first."

Sara says, "Cup with Barney?"

Mom smiles, "Yes, honey, a cup with Barney on it if I can find one. I am going to leave for work pretty soon, but first let me give you a nice big hug."

At this point, I asked my client to describe how he thought the little girl was feeling in this scenario. Was she upset? Was she calm? Len answered, "She was calmer, not so upset." Eureka! We were really starting to get somewhere. These Little Sara vignettes helped Len listen to feelings.

As our work together continued, Len learned how to rediscover and listen to his own feelings, a capability that had been stunted long ago. As we continued to explore other meanings within the Little Sara metaphor, Len started to find better ways to care for and nurture his feeling self, ways that had been sadly abandoned earlier in his life.

Little Sara seemed to have real promise. She was the perfect key for opening up the emotional lock I had encountered with Len. Thinking about her also brought me more in touch with the sense that children come into this world beautifully wired to let us know what they feel and what they need, whether they are frightened, sad, hungry, sleepy, or happy. If we don't mistreat them early on, their unfettered emotions naturally behave like a well-calibrated compass that generally points to true north. Their emotional signal system is nature's way of letting us know what's right and what's not right—if we listen. Properly nurtured, children's feelings provide us with invaluable information for maintaining their emotional and physical well-being. As parents we must closely monitor their emotional signals to detect signs of physical or emotional discomfort or well-being. These signals help us recognize whether our parental actions help or hinder their emotional and physical well-being.

As I worked with the Little Sara metaphor I began to see how a child's emotional signal system does not exist solely to help others promote their emotional and physical well-being. It appears that we have evolved with the capacity to maintain physical and emotional well-being on our own once we have acquired the emotional learning needed to use this system. After realizing this, I decided I might try using Little Sara to facilitate this emotional learning with other clients as well. Little Sara rapidly became my very favorite teacher.

Over and over, Little Sara shows us what works best for her emotionally. We were all born pretty much like her, capable of pointing to true north with our feelings if our feelings are regarded and respected. So, by making Sara any age we want her to be, and by putting her into all kinds of situations, we can quickly determine what's emotionally best for her and most likely us too—because she'll be the first to let us know. She remains absolutely true to her feelings because nobody has messed her up yet. With Little Sara, what you see is what you get. She will let us know straight away if we are heading toward her true north or not. She will also show us that we self-regulate emotions properly only when we are true to our feelings. She will help us see that proper emotional awareness is the royal road to her well-being, as it is to ours. Seeing this connection is the primary objective in this Building Block.

Now let's find out what else Little Sara can tell us about how she should be treated to help keep her emotional health and happiness in good standing. Protecting one's well-being should be a guiding rule with her, and with us. The following vignette is about Sara becoming extremely excited about getting a new puppy. Along the way, we also make sure not to ruin this special occasion by being insensitive to her feelings.

Four-year-old Sara will be getting a new puppy today, and she is so excited that she is literally jumping for joy. At times, she can't seem to restrain herself from leaping up and down with delight. Jumping, and circling at the same time she asks, "Is it time to go yet, can we get the puppy now? Please mommy?"

Mom responds with caring and empathy, "Not quite yet Sara, but soon."

"When mommy, when?" Sara pleads.

"Very soon Sara, in ten minutes or so, just as soon as daddy gets home. I can see just how happy and excited you are, you really want to get our new puppy! I am excited too. We will be leaving to get the puppy very soon but please be patient so we can go as a family."

Sara hugs her mother saying, "I just can't wait to get our puppy."

"I know you can't honey, it's hard for me to wait too."

Here, mom has sensed her daughter's feelings of joy and helps her to sustain it. Sara flourishes.

Compare this validation and understanding of Sara's unbounded enthusiasm with the reply of a different, impatient parental figure we will invent here:

"Look Sara, I am getting tired of all of the noise and commotion you are making over this dog. If it doesn't stop now, we may not go at all."

Sara's elation turns to sullen apprehension. Her fun screeches to a halt. Her capacity to experience elation and excitement is a precious element in her well-being. Dashing her enthusiasm would be a tragic misstep in her nurturance. If we do not support Little Sara's natural excitement, like Len, she too might forget what fun feels like!

Now let's look at how to handle 5½-year-old Sara when she becomes bored. Sara has been entertaining herself in her room for quite a long time, but she has finally reached her limit for finding any other new forms of amusement. She has completely exhausted all of her interesting books, favorite crafts, and stuffed animals; even her tireless imagination has gone on break. Without knowing what else to do, she feels really bored. Sara comes downstairs in frustration, saying to her dad, "I have nothing left to do. Everything here is boring." Happily, her dad is emotionally available and able to hear Sara's signal of distress. Still only a young child, Sara's inability to resolve these kinds of problems on her own is understandable.

Her father replies, "It sounds like you're feeling bored, Sara. You were up in your room a long time. Maybe we need to find something else for you do. We could invite a friend over, go for a walk—or..." prompting Sara a little, "maybe you can think of something else that would be fun to do."

Sara asks, "Can we play a board game? Please daddy?"

Smiling, her father answers, "If you promise not to beat me every time, I guess we can!"

Sara's feelings of boredom are heard and constructively resolved. Her well-being is lovingly rejuvenated.

You can imagine the flip side of this story where Sara's dad is put off by her boredom and doesn't care to listen to her. Imagine also that he acts as though he doesn't want to be bothered by her needs when they arise. Over time, Sara will begin to believe that her feelings don't really matter very much. She will probably start to close down, numb out—like Len did as a child.

In this next scenario, Sara conveys to us that she feels sleepy, although she does not fully recognize that she is tired. Let's keep her at the same age. She is sitting in a big green chair and starting to yawn. As she is talking, her eyes blink and her head nods to the side: she has been a little irritable over the last half hour. Mom reads these signals caringly, saying to Sara, "You know honey, we stayed up pretty late last night and you haven't had your nap yet today. It looks like you may be feeling a little sleepy. A nap might help. Let's go upstairs and I'll lay down with you for a few minutes." Little Sara agrees.

Again, this parent offers the appropriate help and nurturance to Sara. Sara is still a little too young to sense her own needs for rest reliably and sometimes needs the kind of parental nurturance that will best support her well-being in this situation. To Sara's emotional benefit, her mom is careful to listen and communicate to her in a way that will help Sara develop a better understanding of what her feelings mean and what she must ultimately learn to do about them. Good job Sara, good job mom!

Unfortunately, there are many adults who still haven't learned what Sara is learning here. They do not listen well to their own needs and feelings, including their needs for sleep. Other activities like work and business come first on their lists, taking precedence over bodily needs like rest. Too often, well-being becomes the lowest priority. Sadly, this is the lesson that many teach to their children as well.

Sometimes Little Sara's feelings get hurt too. What to do, what to do? Let's conclude by looking into this last example. For this vignette Little Sara is now in second grade. She loves school, but not on this particular day. She's riding home from school on her school bus, sitting next to two of her "friends," Erin and Becky. As you know, kids can be quite mean to each other sometimes. Erin and Becky start to tease Sara about her red curly hair singing, "Your hair looks like carrot juice, your hair looks like carrot juice." They continue chanting, "Your hair looks like carrot juice, your hair looks like carrot juice," even after Sara politely asks them to stop.

Finally, Sara is able to escape the bus. She walks home slowly, head down, entering the kitchen where her mother works on her computer.

Sara's mother greets her, "Hi honey!"

Sara answers flatly, "Hi."

"How was your day?"

Sara, almost inaudibly, replies, "It was OK I guess."

Mom senses otherwise, "It sounds like something's not right; did something happen today?"

Sara's hurt feelings overtake her silence and she blurts out, "They kept saying, 'Your hair looks like carrot juice' over and over. I asked them to stop, but they wouldn't."

"Who said this?"

"Erin and Becky and they kept saying it, over and over."

Sara starts to cry.

"I'm so sorry, Sara. Didn't you tell me Erin and Becky were your friends?"

"Well I guess," she answers, hesitantly.

"You know Sara, that's not the way friends should ever talk to one another—they shouldn't be hurtful like that. I am sorry this happened to you. Let me fix you your snack, and then maybe we can take a walk together with the dog. By the way, Sara, you do have beautiful curly red hair, just like me."

Sara brightens.

The next day, Sara returns from school, a little more bounce in her step. After greeting her, mom asks, "So how are you today?"

Much more animated, Sara says, "Good! I talked to them."

"To whom?"

"Becky and Erin, I told them I didn't like what they said to me yesterday. Friends shouldn't tease each other like that. I said if they wanted to be my friends, they shouldn't do it anymore. They told me they were 'SORREEEE.'"

Way to go Sara. Not too shabby of a performance from this second grader!

First what I want you to see here is that all of us as children, like Little Sara, enter this world well prepared to let others know how we feel. As children, we may not know how to remedy our needs, however, through the expression of feelings and emotions, we signal not only needs like "this bed is too hard," or "my porridge is too hot," but also many other important emotional and physical needs. With proper parental stewardship, our well-being is guarded and strengthened.

We will get the nurturance we need if our parents and other primary caretakers are able to really listen and respond to our physical and emotional needs. Unfortunately, the royal road to happiness and emotional health here has many big "ifs" involved: it works well if family conflict and strife are minimized, and if our parents avoid controlling and overriding our most important feelings, or becoming overly strict. It also only works if our parents aren't excessively needy and if there is no alcoholism or other serious emotional dysfunction in the family. Basically, it will only work if our parents happen to be emotionally available and nurturing to us, each other, and to themselves!

Like Little Sara, all of us are greatly influenced by the positive and negative ways in which those who we love and depend upon treat us. If their nurturing of us has been generally positive and caring, we are likely to be more self-regarding and able to express our feelings. Our well-being is on sound footing. On the other hand, if we are treated negatively—our egos too often weakened by indifference or stung by criticism—we retreat rather than advance, emotionally. We become reluctant to risk further abandonment, hurt, or criticism. Our worth and well-being feel uncertain—each encounter poses another test of whether we are good enough—another test of whether it will be safe enough to just be ourselves, and trust that history won't repeat itself. Sometimes we retreat so far that our real self is no longer present. The self behind the mask is gone; dysfunction abounds.

Even if we did receive the positive nurturing we needed as children, there is something more that we must get to be emotionally complete, able to self-regulate, and able to maintain our emotional well-being. Once our emotional needs have been looked after by our parents, we must then be taught how to self-nurture. We must learn how to take care of our emotional needs on our own. Please note, I did not say we should learn to ignore our feelings or hand this nurturance over for others to do for us, as is too often the case.

Unfortunately, learning to self-nurture is the part of emotional learning that frequently gets missed altogether. If we were among the emotionally fortunate, our parents may have invested a great deal of know-how and energy into nurturing us, but this is still no guarantee that they were proficient at

56

nurturing themselves. Therein lies the paradox. Children learn by example: we must observe what we are to learn. If our parents don't understand and model self-nurturance themselves, we will face very serious challenges learning these behaviors on our own. Despite their best intentions, parents who are really trying their best to love us but lack the ability to self-nurture send us the perplexing message of, "Do as I say, not as I do."

Without ample opportunity to see and learn self-nurturing skills, we are much more likely to evolve into emotionally needy adults who suffer a loss of emotional well-being, or place the burden of our emotional needs on the lives of our significant others. In these instances, our friendships and marriages are prone to be masquerades for what might more properly be called needships. It should come as no surprise that such needships are a real contributing factor to the high divorce rate of today's marriages. Even more concerning, I have become increasingly convinced that many if not most of the widespread behavioral dysfunctions and emotional problems in our society arise from deprivations in parental nurturance and self-nurturance. These deprivations not only disrupt and impair emotional learning, but also contribute to our pervasive problems with dependency and codependency.

Finally, in the interest of protecting our chances for maturing into healthy, self-nurturing adults, I want to mention the potentially pernicious effects of certain cultural scripts embedded in child rearing practices. Examples of common phrases include:

"Big boys don't cry."

"You're acting like a baby."

"You need to grow up."

"Act like a man."

"Act like an adult."

"You're being immature."

While it may be true that some children and adults so accused could be developmentally off their rockers, there is another side to these messages. Namely, the messenger might be saying, "stop showing your real feelings because I don't feel like dealing with them." Or, "act [note: 'act'] like a grown up: i.e. put on your *social mask*, hide your real feelings, and numb out like the rest of us." Here, the exhortations to "grow up" can start us down the slippery slope of learning how to submerge our own feelings and be what somebody else wants, rather than be who we really are. Put on the social mask; act like you aren't feeling what you are feeling (because we're not comfortable expressing how we feel). In trying to meet the requirements of properly wearing our "grown up" social masks we may get too good at practicing the art of being a non-self. A non-self is someone who has learned to submerge his or her identity. If we do this, we are headed down a road to dysfunction. Instead, to grow towards well-being, we must always protect and preserve the wonderful Little Sara within ourselves. We must strive to remain centered, emotionally truthful, and to never lose sight of the person we are inside.

Some Points to Remember

Our feelings provide extremely important information about our physical and emotional well-being. As children, we need to be listened to and nurtured correctly by others in order to prosper and feel well. As we become adults, we must also learn how to perform self-nurturance on our own. For us to have the emotional learning that makes well-being possible, we must receive the right parental nurturing in childhood, or lacking that, we must seek to acquire it later. As Little Sara clearly shows us, she must be loved and nurtured to feel well and flourish. For you to feel well and flourish, you too must make certain that you care for and treat yourself as well as you would her. Be certain that your relationship with yourself—your actions and your ability to self-nurture—pass the Little Sara test: When they would do well by her, then you know they are also right for you.

Study Guide Questions

1. Len did not understand what it meant to listen to himself. What does "listen to yourself" mean?

2. Why is it so important for you to listen carefully to Little Sara and to yourself?

3. Parents need to nurture us and show us how to self-nurture. Explain why both are so important.

4. Many adults appear to be wearing "social masks." What does this behavior suggest?

5. What kinds of things do you think Little Sara is learning through her interactions with the "nice" parental figures in these stories?

6. Explain what "pass the Little Sara test" means in terms of your relationship with yourself.

7. Think about how you would treat Little Sara. How does this compare with how you treat yourself?

5

Building Block 5: Computer Road -
Meet and Greet Freddy

Waiting for Things to happen so you can be happy
is a poor substitute for being happy while you wait
for Things to happen

You already know that your emotions come from your
thoughts and that there are safe and unsafe ways to think about
them. Knowing this gives you a strong advantage in recognizing
where happiness and unhappiness come from. But is that all
there is to it, or is there something more such as a particular way
of thinking—an overall mindset—that lies at the foundation of
emotional well-being? If there is such a mindset, what is it and
what more must you discover and learn about this mindset for
happiness? In this section, you will have a chance to delve into
these matters by witnessing a life-changing experience I had on
Computer Road about 30 years ago.

Looking back, I see that what happened that day provided
me with an invaluable epiphany: it was when I first saw that my
way of conducting "emotional business" only afforded an episodic

and situational version of happiness. Whatever the formula was that might make a person intrinsically happy, if there was such a thing, was missing in me. This unsettling recognition led me to begin my search for a mindset to happiness. I hope that in sharing this personal experience with you, you too will gain some useful insights into your own life.

It was just another workday for me in 1978. I was a couple of minutes into my half-hour drive to work along Computer Road (hence, the name given to this building block) when my thoughts drifted in a way they never had before. For some reason, I asked myself how I was feeling that morning. A seemingly benign question but not a question I would have ordinarily asked myself on a morning ride to work. It was especially out of the ordinary because, at this point in my life, I was a busy young professional heading off to a demanding job as a newly appointed research director: always lots of Things on my mind and Things to be doing. My life was filled with goals to meet and reports to write; I was very busy with Things, little time for emotional chitchats. In my mind, I had lots of important responsibilities to tend to: projects to oversee, graduate students to keep busy, papers to write, and budgets to defend. Did I really have time to answer this question?

Fortunately, I had time on this day. My internal dialogue went something like this:

"How are you feeling right now?"

"Well, I'll tell you how I'm feeling right now—I'm feeling a little stressed out. I have a lot on my plate, a lot expected of me at work and at home; I feel pressured."

"Well, is that it?"

"No, probably not. I worry. It seems like I worry a lot sometimes."

"About what?"

"Lot's of Things I guess—my health for one. My dad died of a heart attack at 32 when I was only five; am I going to die young, like him? I worry about finances, about whether there will be enough money for my family; I worry about my kids, especially their safety. I worry about whether I will live up to the expectations people have for me at work; whether I am smart enough; whether I am nice enough. I worry about a lot of Things. My mom is a worrier, and so was her mother. They all worried a lot. I guess I am a worrier too, like them."

"Are you finished yet or are there other feelings we missed here?

"Well yeah, actually there are. I tend to get angry too much. Things can get me upset pretty easily, and when they do, I torque up. I hate to admit this to myself, but I've probably been like this for a very long time."

"What do you get angry about?"

"My stepfather for one; he was bigoted and very controlling —and he always had a very bad temper. All of this makes me angry."

"Did anything else make you angry a lot?"

"People being mean. My older brother, I suppose. I really like him but he lets me down a lot. I don't feel like I can really trust him to be a nurturing older brother or a good friend."

At the time, I almost couldn't believe what I heard myself saying. The way I was feeling was apparently adding up to something a lot worse than I had imagined. It felt like a tidal wave was rolling over me. One moment I thought Things were good enough or at least, were not that bad; the next minute I thought the opposite.

I felt like saying, "Will the real me please stand up?" Desperate to prove my life wasn't all so bad, I continued my conversation:

"Aren't you ever happy?"

"Of course I am. I was happy when I got married, when we got the house, when the kids were born, when we take vacations, when I got my degree, when we got the dog, at the party the other weekend, whenever I get a paper published. A lot of Things make me feel happy."

But I was also starting to see that maybe it was only when these Things—these events—occurred that I experienced happiness. I began to think, "Maybe most of my happiness is event-based happiness; maybe I'm actually not all that happy most of the time. Maybe I'm only happy around the times when these 'good' Things are happening."

All of this was becoming rather unsettling for me. This was only a half-hour ride to work and my troubles were piling up fast. I felt a vague sinking feeling, why had I gotten into all of this now? Whatever the reasons, I couldn't seem to back away from the thoughts I had started within myself.

"Maybe I was too quick to judge. If I were to look at the question of how I feel, not just through the prism of this morning at this time, but look at my life in a more extended timeframe, maybe then I would see that I'm really a lot happier. Maybe I would see that my life plan is working; that I'm doing OK after all."

"I'll try to take an objective look at the bigger picture: I'm a researcher now and researchers know how to do time samples to get the bigger picture—maybe more data points will help. Suppose I ask myself how I felt every half hour or so, today, yesterday, last week. What would I find? Hopefully, things will look much better then."

My imagination ran with the idea. I asked myself how I felt a half hour before, then an hour before. After some reflection, I found myself answering: "I probably don't feel that much different than how I feel right now. Oh boy, am I in trouble!"

"Well then, what about yesterday? Were those feelings like the troubling ones you have today, or were you able to feel differently, perhaps better?" Playing back the tape of yesterday as best I could, again the answer seemed to be the same: a different day but pretty much the same feelings.

"How about the day before that? There's got to be some light at the end of this tunnel."

Not much different, as best as I could recall.

"And the day before that?"

"The same I guess."

This was not looking good.

In my mind's eye, I saw myself feverishly going through a calendar, looking at all the days that I had just lived and searching for some better ones. I didn't see many. Instead, I saw my hand tearing out most of the pages, one by one, rolling them into small paper balls, and tossing them into a nearby trashcan. I was crashing into the realization that most of these days were not all that happy for me. Would I really wish to relive them as I had if given the chance? No, they would not be "keepers." I tried to push away the disturbing but inevitable conclusion of these thoughts: my life was passing by and I still hadn't found the happiness I thought I would find. I was still waiting to be happy.

The picture was getting grimmer by the moment. Then I hit the real showstopper. A sinking feeling deepened in my chest as my mind realized that I had already tried my very best, played my A game as it were, and I simply hadn't gotten anywhere close to realizing the emotionally satisfying life I thought I would have. I did all the Things I thought I should do: I went to school, got my degrees, worked hard, got married, bought a house in the suburbs and a station wagon, started a family, and was expertly living out my best plan of action for having a happy life, to the letter. However, in the painful light of that morning's reflections, I saw that my life plan was flawed in some fundamental way. I had done all the "right Things" according to my plan. Surely I would become a happier person from all these doings and strivings. But I hadn't. I had earned the pedestal of a successful life, but my sense of happiness was at best, fleeting. I was terribly off course about something, something utterly fundamental. Where had I gone wrong?

In that moment, I truly felt like someone lost in a barren wilderness, unsure about where to turn, almost desperate. The sinking feeling became overwhelming, but desperation sometimes breeds opportunity. Seeing how wrong I had been, I finally heard myself screaming out inside of me, "OK, SO WHAT IS IT THEN THAT A HUMAN BEING NEEDS TO BE TO BE TRULY HAPPY? I HAVE TO FIGURE THIS OUT!"

I was still driving to work but now I was on a mission. Way too much time had been lost in my life. I realized I needed some new ideas because the old ones had gotten me nowhere useful. In my imagination, my researcher mindset kicked back in:

"Maybe I need a study to help me find out what kind of a mindset a person has to achieve in order to have more sustainable happiness. Maybe getting all caught up in chasing the circumstances and Things that I think will make me happy— like I have been—won't ever do it. Following the social script of "doing and getting" my way to a happy life just seems to lead to chasing happiness rather than actually having it."

"There has got to be something better. Suppose I were to focus instead on a person's mindset, on what they need to think or not think; suppose I looked for the right mindset rather than placing so much emphasis on the "right" Things, outside events, and circumstances. Maybe being happy or unhappy starts with how we think about Things."

In the next moment, I imagined myself conducting a study to examine the notion of a mindset for happiness. I just needed to find a good representative of the human species so I could probe into this mindset-for-happiness idea. To complete this mental exercise, I dreamt up a "subject" for a study who I now fondly refer to as Freddy. I decided I would describe different scenarios to Freddy in order to stir up his thinking, hopefully exposing the basis for a happiness mindset. I hoped he would show me when his mindset felt right and when it did not, perhaps giving me a better perspective.

At this point, you might be thinking that I just made all of this up for the book. Fortunately, I didn't—that day shaped my thoughts in a lasting way that I am simply recounting to you now. Some thoughts have been updated and clarified, but it is otherwise unadulterated. A 30-minute ride to work can be just long enough to force some important questions. What a day!

Continuing with the study I was imagining, I said to a research colleague assisting me, "Mike, please bring our subject in and ask him to be seated," as I stood behind a one-way mirror, watching.

"OK, good," using an intercom audible only to my associate, "please give the subject a warm greeting. Help him to feel accepted and tell him how grateful we are that he could participate in this important study. Now ask him how he feels."

My associate reports, "He says he likes feeling accepted."

"OK, good. I should write this down: 'subject likes feeling accepted.' Don't want to forget it! Now please tell him we picked him because we felt he will make an outstanding subject for our study. Let him know how valued he is. How does he feel about that?"

"He says he likes hearing that."

"OK, I had better write this down too: 'likes feeling valued.' Now let's see what he says when he feels disappointed. Mike, please tell Freddy we had planned on giving him a nice gift card of $300 to Borders for his participation today, but we aren't now because I decided to use the money for a staff party instead. How does he feel?"

"He says he feels bad now," Mike answers. "He doesn't like feeling disappointed."

"Alright, I've got to write this down, 'subject does not like feeling disappointed.' I must not forget this. Maybe we are getting somewhere with this guy. Let's compliment him and see what happens. Tell him he has a really great personality and a great tan going on."

"He says he's feeling good after hearing that."

"OK, 'likes compliments, got it.' What about worries? Certainly worrying was something I and other members of my family of origin were experts at doing. Let's see, oh yeah, ask our subject if that is his blue convertible over in the corner of our parking lot. Tell him it looks like somebody might have just side-swiped it."

"The subject tells us that he's really upset about his car now and he really doesn't like feeling so worried like this."

"OK, thanks Mike, 'our subject doesn't like being worried,' got it. Quickly, maybe we'd better tell him something reassuring...um, we are mistaken; it was the car next to his."

"He's says he's feeling a lot better now. He's glad to hear Things are OK."

"Writing it down! 'Prefers thinking Things are OK.' Now let's tell him a good joke."

"He's laughing! He really enjoyed the joke."

"Making another note now, 'likes having funny thoughts.' What if he starts thinking he's not good enough? Suggest to the subject that we are now having some doubts about whether he is as representative of the human species as we hoped. Maybe he's not good enough. How is he feeling now?"

"Not good at all, Bob. He's quite sad now."

"Got it Mike, better write this one down too, 'does not like thinking he is inadequate.'"

I was nearing the end of my drive to work. Mike asked me a question about the study with Freddy. "Alright," he said, "suppose we are able to find out what people like to feel and what they don't like feeling from this guy. So what then? How do we make ourselves feel the way we want to? How can we make ourselves feel happy without always having to change the circumstances around us?" I heard myself answer, "Mike, one step at a time. Maybe we first need to know in what ways we need to think to feel happy. Then maybe we can try to figure out

70

how to make ourselves think and feel this way. I think we just have to take this one step at a time, and see what we can do."

Later that day on my way home from work I thought some more about my epiphany. Perhaps I needed to develop a better mindset for happiness. What could I do that would make Freddy feel happy? I had been doing some reading in the area of self-management theory. Some psychologists were talking about how you could use behavior modification principles on yourself. For example, you could use positive reinforcement on yourself to help with a dieting plan or as a reward for exercising. Could I try modifying my thoughts to enhance my emotional well-being? I do not believe the self-management people were actually suggesting this at the time, but I thought this idea might be worth a try. What did I have to lose? I picked a thought pattern that "my subject" liked having—a compliment—Freddy liked compliments.

I realized that I rarely complimented myself. In fact I was hard on myself most of the time. When I wasn't putting myself down, I was waiting for others to compliment me. Sometimes I seemed to go out of my way for people, quietly hoping I would get some much-needed recognition. Lacking in the ability to acknowledge myself, I generally relied on the feelings of others for my approval and self-esteem. I often felt disappointed if others failed to compliment me and became overly sensitive when they were critical. I wondered, 'suppose I deliberately increase self-compliments.' I reckoned any increase would be a big improvement. Would I be able to make myself feel better, feel happier? Given the bad news I had gotten earlier in the day about being way off course on my plans for becoming happy, even a long shot like this was worth a try.

At first, it was hard to even think of a good compliment I could tell myself. Finally, after a lot of searching, I came up with the brilliant idea to tell myself that I had nice blond hair. All right, I know how pathetic this sounds, but I had to do something and this is the best I could come up with. I was in unchartered waters, but I was determined.

I thought about this complimentary thought a number of times each day, giving myself a cue to remember to do it. I monitored how I felt and noticed that changing my thinking like this did create a positive feeling. I was certainly a long way from a new mindset, but it was a beginning. I started to wonder what other possibilities this approach could open up.

A great deal more as it turns out. This was not only the first step in modifying my own happiness behavior, more importantly it was also the first step in laying down a foundation for the way I now live my life and define my approach to psychotherapy. It was also the first among many steps that have led to the conceptualization and writing of this book. Living and teaching a straightforward cognitive behavioral system that promotes self-nurturance, happiness and emotional well-being is now a rewarding and consuming life passion for me. This day on Computer Road became permanently life altering.

Some Points to Remember

To acquire the requisite knowledge for happiness and emotional well-being, we must receive proper nurturing. Sometimes, what we learn works against our needs for emotional health and happiness, rather than for them. We feel sad too frequently, don't like ourselves enough, worry too often, and lose out too much on being happy. When this happens, feeling well is challenging, and happiness is, at best, sporadic. We muddle our way along with these challenges, relying on substitutions to ramp up our well-being, or worse yet, we wind up suffering with more serious emotional problems. I hope that my story points us in a better direction—toward finding a mindset for happiness. As you will see, learning this mindset is a most fruitful path for being happy and staying well.

Study Guide Questions

1. What does event-based happiness refer to? What is the problem with this approach to happiness?

2. What, if any, connections to your own life can you draw from the Computer Road story?

3. Why couldn't I trust my old way of thinking about what made me happy?

4. What is the intended meaning of a mindset for happiness?

5. What did you conclude from the experiment with Freddy?

6

Building Block 6: The Red Deer Story

The love we are not given, we must learn how to give to ourselves

What happens to Little Sara or any of us if we are denied the good fortune of being reared in an emotionally healthy, nurturing family? What happens to us? What options do we have? As children, not all of us were blessed with stable, loving environments. The red deer story explores this question.

I am driving home from the office about 15 years ago, listening to the "science Friday guy" on National Public Radio. Two researchers were discussing an interesting behavior pattern they had studied in red deer. In observing herds of red deer, they found that these animals were "group decision makers," that is, they seemed to use a group decision-making process as a way of determining whether to go or stay put. When several animals stood up to leave, the herd would follow only if a majority also "assented" by standing up to go. Otherwise they would remain seated or sit back down, and the herd would go nowhere. Generally, between 60 and 70 percent of the deer would need to "rise in favor" if the herd was going to go anywhere. The herd, for better or for worse, determined the herd's fate.

As I reflected on this behavior, I marveled at how a tactic as complicated as democracy had emerged from years of natural experimentation in these deer. By behaving in unison, rather than playing follow the leader, the herd was attempting to afford their kind a safer journey to food, water, shelter and continued survival. Whatever the case, since the red deer are still with us, I reasoned that they must have been doing something right.

Still reflecting on these adaptive mechanisms, my mind started thinking about "the human herd." "We humans herd also," I thought, "not exactly as deer in herds, but in social units meant to protect us. We herd in tribes, communes, other social collectives, and in families. Just one more of nature's evolutionary experiments that has helped us humans to get from there to here," I concluded. We are meant to herd it seems, perhaps herding protects us. The family would be our most basic herding unit. Certainly the family is one of nature's most important resources for helping each of us receive the nurturance we need to grow, survive, and prosper. I had rediscovered the obvious I guess, but I had also reached a new perspective. I was done thinking about all of this and turned up the volume on my car radio, contented with my reflections, and continued my drive home. I was done with the human herd theory—or so I thought.

It was probably six or seven weeks later when a whole new twist to this story developed. On this day, I found myself telling my wife about the red deer, recounting for her almost the exact same circumstances I have just described for you. But suddenly, and I always seem to feel a deep stirring of emotion when I get to this part of the narrative, I said to my wife: "I left the herd; I felt I had to pull back." Of course she immediately asked me what in the world I was talking about. Apparently without realizing it, I had done a lot more thinking about the red deer business, and it was all about to start pouring out of me.

My words were rapid, "Look, look at what happened in my family. After my dad died, it was just we three kids and mom. Then my stepfather came onto the scene. He was so controlling, verbally abusive and angry with us a lot of the time. The home environment was extremely hard on Bruce (my older brother) and June (my younger sister) too. Mom tried to stand up for us, but my stepfather wore her down over time. She was very kind to us, but a worrier and unassertive. It seemed as though we had to like what he liked, see things the way he did, not really be ourselves. Bruce, June and I would be complaining to one another about our stepfather again and again. We felt stuck in a very toxic situation that we were powerless to control. Finally, when I left for graduate school, although away from my family, I actually started to feel better. My hurt, my anger, my sadness lessened.

"I was away, but my brother and sister were not. Even though they too were troubled about the home situation, they stayed nearby. They seemed to feel guilty about doing otherwise. They were stuck in the herd. At times, I heard I should also be there like them—as bad as it was. I resisted the guilt, theirs and

77

my own, as best I could. It wasn't easy for me, but I stayed away
a lot. They stayed with the herd—the unhealthy herd, but I left!

"I had gotten away. Maybe distancing myself from the
day-to-day privations of living at home would give me a better
chance to work out some things. It would take time, but at least
I could start looking at my life more clearly. I wouldn't be
constantly exposed to the emotional wounding. I could find out
why I was not very happy at times, and what I might do to resolve
it.

"Being away from the herd was also difficult, certainly no
guarantee that things would be better, but it gave me a chance to
sort some things out. Eventually, I was able to do a lot of sorting.
Bruce and June stayed with the herd. I think, out of guilt and
necessity, they felt they had to. But look, look what happened to
them. Neither of them got the chance, nor found a way of
becoming emotionally whole, especially Bruce. Bruce developed a
life-long alcohol problem. He had three very troubled marriages,
and lived in a world of narcissism and compulsion. He never
became emotionally well. June managed to fair somewhat better,
but she too has carried the wounds of our childhood, and
struggles with depression and emotional vulnerability."

I had never seen the effects of our family circumstances so
clearly. The enormous dilemma that we all faced: to stay and
risk the suffering and emotional impoundment implicit in the
day-to-day attachment to our wounded family, or to leave. In
leaving, to lose the fantasized hope of family support and
nurturance, and to face the guilt and uncertainty inherent in

pulling away. What is a person to do when their herd is sick? I felt sadness for them and for all of us. Perhaps there was some better alternative, but we did not find it.

For me, the deepest meaning in this red deer story is seeing and somehow facing this dilemma, seeing that the choices we face in these circumstances can be difficult as well as life-determining. To feel well, we must find the path whereby we can learn how. The path through our family was blocked. The help we all needed was not made available.

When there is willingness and help available, or the problems in the family are not too severe, maybe better solutions can be found that help avoid the challenging dilemma of staying or leaving. Too often, however, people living in these family situations get caught up in emotional traps. They get trapped in their own hurt and resentments about how their family has treated them over the years, or in the illusion that the love and nurturance they have been missing and longing for will somehow magically come about on its own, if they just try a little harder or wait a little longer. These traps forestall moving forward. Whatever choice we make in these circumstances, even if it might sometimes mean leaving the herd, we must try to search out a path that will lead us toward emotional well-being.

Some Points to Remember

Although we all need to receive proper nurturing to become physically and emotionally healthy adults, not all of us are blessed with family circumstances that can fulfill this need.

Most parents do the best they can with what they know, but this by no means assures that we will gain the emotional resources we need to become well and happy adults. To grow up well naturally, yes, our parents must nurture us well. But then they must also teach us how to be self-nurturing, so that we prosper and learn how to prosper on our own. But our opportunities to learn these skills through our families and primary caretakers are not always perfect. We must try to fill in the imperfections.

Study Guide Questions

1. What are some potential risks of staying connected to an "unhealthy herd"?

2. What is the major dilemma facing those who are in a dysfunctional family?

3. Do you see any connections between the red deer story and your life growing up with your family of origin? Briefly elaborate.

4. If we did not receive the love we needed, what must we learn to do?

7

Building Block 7: Widgets for Improving Thinking

Your thoughts should be working for you; you
shouldn't be working for them

From what you have read, I am sure you are beginning to
appreciate just how critical your patterns of thinking are in
determining both what you feel and how well you feel. Your
thinking, specifically your safe versus unsafe thoughts, shapes
the feelings and emotions you experience as well as your overall
mood. Knowing how to choose and change your thinking is
particularly important because it enables you to steer your
feelings in the direction you want them to go, no matter how you
may have learned to think in your past. Instead of being
situation-bound, you will gain direct control over your mood and
your emotional well-being. In the following section, you will learn
more about specific tools, or "widgets", that you can use to lessen
unsafe thinking, increase safe thinking, and improve your
happiness. Because these widgets are powerful techniques for
managing your thoughts and feelings, I would strongly encourage

you to commit them to memory before continuing to later Building Blocks.

In this Building Block, you will learn about three thought management techniques that will help you to reduce unsafe thinking: *thought stopping, thought shifting,* and *cognitive restructuring.* You will also learn several techniques you can use to increase safe thinking. These techniques are: *positive noticing, positive affirmations* and *stockpiling.*

First, let's review some techniques for dealing with disturbing or unsafe thinking. As you recall, unsafe thinking brings certain disturbing feelings, whether these emotions emanate from fearful thinking, worry, angry thinking, regret or some other type of negative thinking. These thoughts stir up the kind of feelings that make us feel bad and diminish our emotional contentment. Sometimes we justify feeling negative emotions for a period of time by telling ourselves our feelings are "totally appropriate to the situation" or "only natural," as often occurs during bereavement. However, if we stay in these negative thinking states for too long, we can wind up hindering readjustment to the situation. All too often there is really no good reason or benefit behind our penchants for unsafe thinking.

Thought Stopping

When you want to get rid of the disturbing feelings that become stirred up by your unsafe thinking, one approach is thought stopping. Thought stopping is pretty much what it sounds like; it is stopping the thought or thoughts you have that

84

give rise to negative feelings. So, for example, if Ellen is feeling worried and anxious about whether the nice man she met two evenings ago is ever going to call her back again, she could try using this thought stopping technique to eliminate her feelings of uneasiness. Specifically, she could shut off her unsafe thinking by deciding not to keep thinking her worrisome thoughts about this situation, and thereby help herself to stop feeling worried and anxious. All she really needs to do is stop this negative, unsafe thinking.

Thought stopping unsafe thinking sounds pretty simple, and ultimately it is. However, I can't tell you how many times I've heard people say, "That's not going to be easy for me to do." I remind them that the only real truth in this perspective is that if they believe that it will be hard to stop what they think, indeed it *will* be hard. *I want you to reflect on this important point again: by believing in the stubbornness of negative thoughts, you actually make it harder to stop having them. Always remember: what you think is what you get!* The first step is to decide who you want running the show, you, or some self-defeating thought that interferes with your state of happiness? If you think you can't do something, you won't. If you think maybe you can, maybe you will. If you teach yourself to think that you can turn off unsafe thinking, then that is what you will be able to do.

The importance of knowing that we are supposed to be the one in charge of our own thinking was smartly summed up in the comment made by an eight-year-old client I had the pleasure of working with. Her father had come in with her one day wanting to know more about what we had been working on that accounted for this little girl's noticeable improvement. I answered him by going over a few of the treatment goals she and I had been working on together.

As I was concluding, the little girl said to us, "Dr. Bob, I think there is something very important you forgot to mention." I asked her what that was. She replied, "You forgot to tell my father that my thoughts work for me; I don't work for them." Her razor sharp understanding left us both practically speechless. As she showed by elegantly rephrasing my suggestions, she had a firm grasp of this important idea. She understood that she should be the one in charge of her thoughts, not the other way around. Her understanding and use of this knowledge became a major reason for her progress in therapy and her success has reinforced my optimism that the rest of us are able to master our thinking too. Fire your unsafe thinking!

Thought stopping is an extremely useful tool for managing your emotions. *Please try practicing this technique now. Practice turning on an unsafe thought, a worry thought for example. Now stop the thought, turn it off, and repeat this on-off sequence several more times so you get used to doing it.* As you do this, you strengthen your ability to thought-stop and control your negative feelings.

Because unsafe thinking is so often an unproductive, energy-wasting pattern of behavior that thwarts a positive outlook on life and diminishes emotional health and well-being, it is essential to put the brakes on this thinking promptly. As we

86

learned in Building Block 3, unsafe thoughts are a signal for action, not a state to stay in. One of the reasons why people engage in a lot of unsafe, drama-producing thinking is that they believe that what they think about is necessarily true. Something is bad so they should feel bad. For example, the dishwasher stopped working and we *should* be mad or upset that this happened, or we have a doctor's appointment to go to and we *should* be worried about it. A more practical, and far less self-disturbing way of looking at these events is to think, "I could make myself upset about this situation, but I choose not to. The reason I am going to avoid thinking unsafely is because I don't want to make these situations worse for myself by thinking poorly and negatively about them. No matter what, none of these situations will feel as bad if I decide to stop myself from thinking badly about them." As I tell my clients, "most of the worst experiences in my life never actually happened; they only occurred somewhere between my left and right ear."

Even when you are asked to look at your problems in this way, you may hear yourself saying, "Sounds all well and good, but I can't just make myself think differently like this." But yes, you can. To help yourself, think of it in this way: if I asked you to stick your hand into a pot of scalding hot water, I am sure you could most definitely get yourself to think, "Absolutely not." The reason is straightforward. You correctly see (i.e., think) something like, "I would never do that because that would really hurt me." And you are absolutely right! By the same token, when you needlessly let yourself stay in a state of unsafe thinking, you are also engaging in behavior that is hurtful. You are hurting yourself with your own disturbing thoughts. The main point is this: although there are many reasons and excuses we give ourselves for continuing to engage in unsafe thinking, there are *very few* good reasons for doing it. By looking at your unsafe thinking from this perspective, you will give yourself the right motivation to stop your unsafe thinking.

Thought Shifting

Another thought management technique, somewhat related to thought stopping, is known as thought shifting. The idea behind thought shifting is to redirect your thoughts away from a disturbing topic and on to a safer thought—*not* to another disturbing one! The purpose behind thought shifting is to give your mind something else to focus on, something refreshing, beneficial. For example, if Ed finds himself worrying about not being tall enough, he might decide to shift his thinking to something else, such as how great his new haircut looks. Using thought shifting, Ed stops thinking negatively about something he can't change, and elects to think about something better, in this case, something that he does have control over. Although Ed has not grown any taller, he sure feels happier. Thought shifting is a very useful widget for helping us curb unsafe thinking by finding something more positive to think about. Remember to think, "This negative thought is dragging me down and hurting me. Why am I hurting myself? This is not a good thing for me to do. I am going to stop now. Instead, I am going to think about something to do and do it soon".

Cognitive Restructuring

Sometimes we find that we are caught up in unsafe, misery-generating thinking despite our best efforts to make this thinking go away. It feels as though "we just can't help it." The bad thinking just keeps popping up again and again as we try to push it away. Even when we try thought stopping or thought shifting, nothing helps. The bad ideas seem to win, taking on a life of their own. We need something stronger to get rid of the negative thoughts, something like a thought-cleansing agent with the power of Mr. Clean to help us permanently get rid of persistent negative thinking. Well, there is also a widget for this kind of job. It is called cognitive restructuring.

First popularized by Albert Ellis (1975), cognitive restructuring is a thought-changing tool that is especially good for getting rid of our stubborn, self-disturbing, and irrational thoughts and beliefs. Ellis's use of the term "irrational belief" is similar to "unsafe thinking," it refers to thinking that serves little if any purpose; unjustifiable ways of thinking that simply make us feel bad. To employ cognitive restructuring you first zero in on the self-disturbing thinking that causes you to feel bad. You set about disputing the validity of this thinking by convincing yourself to see that this irrational way of looking at things is wrongly and needlessly causing you to feel disturbed. You then change or restructure your thinking to a more rational viewpoint that no longer incorporates these self-disturbing elements.

To see how cognitive restructuring is applied, let's review an example. Steve has decided to take a graduate course in statistics (poor Steve!). After getting a score of 74 on his first exam he begins getting down on himself, wondering why he even decided to go to graduate school in the first place. He tells me he studied really hard for the test and he did the best that he could do, but getting this "awful test score" has made him begin to feel "like a loser." Even though he has usually gotten good grades in his other courses, and has always done well in school, he has now begun to lose motivation for studying. The fact that Steve's grade in statistics has led him to think of himself as "a loser," indicates that he is engaging in some irrational (very unsafe), self-disturbing thinking about his performance in this statistics class. Steve needs to see that by thinking this way—by irrationally getting down on himself and telling himself he's a loser—he is needlessly disturbing himself and weakening his motivation to study. To get back on track Steve needs to challenge his negative thinking and rid himself of thoughts that label him as a loser and encourage him to want to give up. He must restructure his thinking so that it is not disturbing and fatalistic, reminding himself that his grade in statistics may be a small setback, but it is certainly not the end of the world or a reason to give up. He also needs to tell himself that he is a very good and conscientious student who should never think of himself as a loser over a temporary setback in his performance.

Even in the unlikely instance that he did not wind up doing well in this statistics course, he could take another course or apply himself elsewhere, but under no circumstance would it ever be good to view himself as a loser. By using this cognitive restructuring approach, Steve can dismantle his negative thinking and replace it with more constructive thinking, thereby improving his mood, and his ability to move forward again with his schoolwork.

Just as these thought changing widgets can help you to get rid of negative, unsafe thinking, there are others that can help you to increase positive, safe thinking. Remember the point that was made earlier: reducing emotional disturbance does not, in itself, produce high levels of emotional well-being. To elevate health and happiness to their fullest, we also need to encourage and sustain safe thinking. Elevating your safe thinking directly improves your mood—and it involves no medication! The emotional quality of each and every moment in your life is largely determined by what you are thinking at that moment. When it comes to your emotional well-being, an important part of the job is keeping your thinking safe across these moments. In the material that follows, you will find out about techniques that will help you do this.

Positive Noticing

I refer to a very good strategy for increasing your positive feelings and mood as positive noticing. As the name implies, positive noticing is focusing on the positive aspects of your world.

When you use this technique, you feed your mind information that is emotionally uplifting. One way you can do this is by looking around your environment to admire various aspects of it, for example, your beautiful cat resting in the sun at the window, or the succulent aroma of stew simmering on the stove, the fantasia of moon shadows on a fresh snowfall, the great look of your new sweater, or how cozy it feels on you, the smell of homemade chocolate chip cookies baking in the oven. All of these mood-elevating observations and millions more, are free for the taking. Each and every one of these thoughts serves to deepen your satisfaction of the moment. Of course, scanning your environment is just a way of giving yourself cues to help elicit positive thinking. You can also stimulate safe thinking through reflection and meditation, by guiding your thoughts into positive areas. You will learn more about this when we discuss stockpiling.

To gain the benefit of positive noticing, you simply need to remain mindful of noticing things in a way that helps you to generate mood-enhancing thoughts. If not, you could easily get sidetracked on another problem, something we all seem too prone to do. We are prone to notice everything that is wrong, broken, undone, or problematic in a disquieting way that generates feelings of uneasiness and disturbance. Positive noticing provides a nice relief from the problem-centered mindset that is easily evoked by the stresses of modern life. Now, please take a moment to positively notice. What do you see or hear or smell that you like? Savor it, and notice how this makes you feel.

Strive to make positive noticing something you do throughout each and every day.

Positive Affirmations

Positive affirmations also generate safe thinking. Affirmations are positive ideas and beliefs that you can create and use to foster personal confidence, security, esteem, and relaxation as well as other important psychological states. As such, when you endorse and use these ideas, you give yourself another excellent strategy for boosting your mood and enhancing your emotional well-being. By engaging these affirmations in your thoughts, you increase your ability to feel and act in ways that are beneficial to you. For example, by encouraging yourself to endorse an affirmation like "I am a good speaker," you can help to feel more comfortable about speaking before groups and help yourself get better at doing it. Saying to yourself, "I strive to be a good person" will not only help you feel good about yourself, it will also help you to act in this way. Good ideas and beliefs are the wellspring of good feelings and behaviors. Replacing a self-doubting belief such as "I don't like how I look" with a positive one such as, "I am comfortable with my looks," or better yet, "I like how I look," is a straightforward application of a positive affirmation which will help us to feel better about ourselves.

But a word of caution is needed here. If someone is telling him or herself, in a Pollyanna fashion, that they look fine when they are seriously obese and endangering their health and possibly their life with their weight problem, this individual would be dangerously abusing the purpose of this strategy. You don't want to use these positive affirmations to evade reality. You want to use them to help you feel happier and cope better with reality. Thus, thinking more confidently beats self-doubt and helps us feel and be more confident.

Where might the use of these positive affirmations help bolster your well-being? ***Stop and ask yourself if you see a particular problem area in your own thinking that tends to diminish your feelings of well-being. Write an affirmation that would improve your thinking in this area. Once you decide on the new affirmation, practice this new way of thinking on a daily basis until it becomes part of your belief system. Oh yes, one more thing, affirm that your emotional health and happiness are important to you and keep reading this book to prove it!***

Stockpiling

The next safe thinking widget I want you to know how to use I have termed stockpiling. The essence of stockpiling is to build up an inventory of good ideas and safe thinking. It's easier to create a good meal when you have all the right ingredients, and it is also easier to create a good mood when you have the right safe thoughts. In this instance, by stockpiling your favorite thoughts, you can build up a superb inventory of ideas that will engender positive feelings and well-being every time you engage them. Notice that you don't necessarily have to go somewhere, or get something or do anything to engender a positive mood. What you do have to do is think about things in ways that promote your happiness and contentment.

By stockpiling your favorite thoughts from your memories and experiences, from cherished moments, from your favorite imaginings and fantasies, you can give yourself a vast supply of good ingredients for safe thinking and personal happiness. You can buy a new blouse to make yourself feel good, but you can also think and feel well about the one you are wearing, or one you loved wearing, or one you might own and wear someday. It's nice to have lots of options besides having to always do something, to keep yourself happy. Remember, it wasn't so much what you did that made you happy in the first place; it was what you thought about it that did. So build your stockpile of good thoughts, keep adding new inventory, and keep using this treasure trove in your thinking every day.

When you read Building Blocks 9 and 10, you will learn about some additional, very powerful, thought-changing techniques that you can use to build up the core foundational thinking and beliefs that are essential for your emotional well-being to last longer. I call these widgets six-step plans. These six-step plans will give you systematic, step-by-step guides for restructuring some core parts of your thinking through the use of "corrective cognitions." These six-step plans are great "power tools" for making your mindset become a strong mindset for self-esteem, happiness and well-being.

Because our good intentions for behavior change and self-improvement, like many New Year's Eve resolutions, often fall by the wayside, we need to use reliable methods—clear, systematic, doable plans of action—to help us realize these intentions. Incorporating clear, specific behavioral steps that promote the right follow-through for behavioral change to occur, these six-step plans offer reliable methods for insuring self-improvement. Learning and actually using these six-step plans will not only inspire you to have greater confidence in your ability to change your thinking and behavior, they will also improve your success rate in making important behavioral changes that lead to improvements in well-being.

These widgets are good to know about, but I don't want you to leave it at that. *"Know" means "do" here!* Only when you actually *do* what you are learning about, i.e. begin using these widgets regularly to foster your safe thinking, will you gain the benefits for your personal happiness. Start using these widgets now!

Some Points to Remember

Changing your thinking is not all that difficult, especially if you don't think that it will be. By knowing how to change your thinking, you will be giving yourself the power to control your mood and happiness more directly. The widgets are excellent tools that will help you reduce your negative thinking and increase your positive thinking. By choosing to use these thought changing tools regularly, you will be taking a major step forward toward building your mindset for a happier and emotionally healthier you.

Study Guide Questions

1. Name three techniques for reducing unsafe thinking.

2. In what way are *thought stopping* and *thought shifting* the same? How do they differ?

3. Give two examples of *positive noticing.*

4. Explain the idea behind stockpiling. How do you intend to use this tool?

5. Why is it so important for you to know and use these widgets?

6. Outline a plan to change a negative thinking pattern that you have by using cognitive restructuring.

8

Building Block 8: The Ideal Friend Exercise

When we are nurtured by others, we have well-being for today; when we learn how to self-nurture, we have well-being for a lifetime

You are now ready to address the central premise of this book: how to create a mindset for enduring happiness and emotional well-being. In this chapter, you will learn about a model of thinking that facilitates self-nurturance and the proper mindset for intrinsic happiness. You will be introduced to this model by way of the *Ideal Friend Exercise*. The discussion following the exercise will explain why the nurturance we envision through the Ideal Friend Exercise is universally important to us emotionally, and why developing a mindset for self-nurturance that is deeply rooted in these nurturing ideals affords us a powerful strategy for emotional wellness and happiness.

In Building Block 9, "Creating the Mindset for Emotional Well-Being", you will learn how and where you can change and restructure your thinking so that your mind is guided by the principles that best promote and sustain your emotional wellness. You will get to use a six-step plan to insure that you have the proper motivation for self-nurturance and personal happiness. You will also find out about a great shortcut that will make developing this new mindset much easier for you.

In Building Block 10, you will have opportunity to work on strengthening the specific emotional habits that form the basis of your mindset for well-being, using more of these six-step behavior changing techniques. After completing this material, you will have the essential understanding, motivation, and emotional tools—the essential emotional learning— for sustaining a more joyful state of mind

The Ideal Friend Exercise

The emotional knowledge and understanding you have already gained through the building block discussions give you a good foundation for completing these last important steps in our journey together. You know, for example, that your feelings come from your thoughts rather than from Things outside of you (Building Block One). You also know that the types of thinking you let yourself engage in (Safe versus Unsafe) have a major influence in determining whether your feelings and mood states are positive or negative. Next, you found out that nature has provided you with an emotional signal system to assist you in maintaining your physical and emotional well-being. Thanks to Little Sara, you see how nurturing her well is what will keep her well and, most importantly, you are aware that the best way to treat her is also the best way to treat you. On Computer Road you found out how a person (me for sure) can believe they are doing all the right Things yet come to see that that their happiness is only intermittent and far less than they envisioned. You also got introduced to Freddy on our trip down Computer Road. He showed us that some mindsets are definitely more conducive to emotional health and contentment than others. You found out how Freddy's feelings could be moved in a more positive direction by changing his mindset and getting him to think right. Through the Red Deer Story, you can see that if circumstances fated us to be raised in a herd that is emotionally unhealthy, we are unlikely to get the nurturing we need. Our ability to self-nurture will be compromised and our needs to find emotional well-being will be more pressing and more challenging. We must find other ways to correct nature's imperfections for ourselves. Finally, you acquired some useful thought-changing widgets to help you directly change and improve how you think and feel. Now, you are ready to take the final and most important steps for achieving enduring happiness and well-being for yourself, steps, which help you create the mindset for happiness. You will begin with the Ideal Friend Exercise.[6]

The Ideal Friend Exercise is a cognitive behavior technique I designed to help you build a sound mindset for happiness and emotional well-being. I began using this technique many years ago as a way of helping my clients learn how to switch their self-disturbing thought patterns to more positive ways of thinking. During the course of my work I became convinced that when

---

[6] I wish to acknowledge the work of Louis Proto (1993) whose seminal thinking on being a 'best friend' to ourselves helped inspire the development of this exercise.

people are shown how to restructure their mindset so that nurturing and emotionally beneficial types of thinking guide it, their mental health and well-being vastly improve. Teaching people how to feel well seemed so much more rewarding than just helping them control symptoms and reduce disturbance. This became the focus of my therapeutic work.

The material you are reading in this book aligns closely with the aims of Positive Psychology, which consider human happiness and well-being a central focus. The Positive Psychology Movement, spearheaded by the work of Martin Seligman at the University of Pennsylvania, has expanded rapidly over the last decade (Seligman, 2002; Snyder & Lopez, 2002). Growing disillusionment with the traditional fixations on mental illness and psychological disturbance has helped spawn this proactive trend. More recent thinking suggests that psychological science needs to go in a direction that promotes better answers for raising the quality of human experience and enhancing emotional wellness. The Positive Psychology Movement has brought well-being and happiness to the fore and established them as worthy and necessary pursuits.

The model of thinking you will be learning how to use is also strongly rooted in the concepts and principles of Cognitive Behavioral Therapy. As such, it draws heavily upon cognitive behavioral theory and research that emphasizes the importance of thoughts and beliefs as key determinants of human feelings and actions. Over the last several decades, research and practice in the field of Cognitive Behavioral Therapy have resulted in a vast accumulation of psychological knowledge and the promulgation of many new and effective techniques for treating a broad range of mental health problems. While this work has revolutionized the nature and scope of psychological service interventions, much of it has stayed with the more limited focus of eliminating symptoms and behaviors associated with emotional disturbance. The development of well-defined cognitive behavioral formulations that help people increase their happiness and emotional health still lag well behind.

Through the Ideal Friend Exercise, you will be introduced to a cognitive behavioral model that helps you better recognize and understand the most important core beliefs for emotional well-being. By focusing on the positive aspects of mental health and well-being, rather than symptoms of disturbance, this model concentrates the purpose of psychological change on learning how to think and feel well rather than reducing signs of mental disturbance through symptom management. The Ideal Friend Exercise clarifies and defines the mindset that will help you create and maintain the positive emotions that are essential for good mental health and more lasting happiness. By going through the Ideal Friend Exercise with me now, you will be on your way to creating this mindset.

We begin this exercise with a very important first step: asking yourself to think about the characteristics of an ideal friend. I could, of course, just tell you what I think an ideal friend is, but doing so would not be very helpful to you. It is important for you to think about this idea first so that you get in touch with your own thinking about the subject. In your mind, what are the most important characteristics or qualities of an ideal friend? Notice that I am not just asking you to define the qualities of a good friend. I want you to aim high here, really high, as high as you possibly can. Imagine the very best friend you can think of—the ideal friend.

As an example, a characteristic that your ideal friend might possess is that he or she is loyal. 'Fun to be around' might be another quality your ideal friend would possess. As you think of these characteristics, make a list of them in your notes at the back of this book. It does not matter whether this ideal friend is a person who actually exists. However, if you do have someone in mind that seems to possess many of these qualities, you can use this person as a reference point for developing your ideas. What matters most is that your list contains all of the qualities that you think are really important for being an ideal friend.

Most of these qualities or characteristics can be written in one word or in a short phrase. Each characteristic should be a separate idea. Please avoid using any compound sentences or paragraphs when writing down these characteristics. Since we will be reviewing them one by one later on, making each of your ideas clear and separate from the others will make it easier. Write down each characteristic, creating a bulleted list.

How many of these characteristics should you have? This can vary, but between 15 and 20 should probably suffice because these qualities should be broad and general. Thirty or more begins to go over the top. You can select a characteristic you would want in this ideal friend or characteristics you would not want in this ideal friend. Wherever possible, however, try to express the characteristic as a positive trait. For example, "My ideal friend is 'honest' as opposed to 'not a liar.'"

Using the note pages in the back, please begin working on your ideal friend list now. Do not worry about whether your list is "correct" or not. Your job right now is to dig inside of yourself and decide what is best—best in terms of how someone should treat you, or you them. *Very important: Do not skip over this part of the exercise or read ahead before completing your ideal friend list.*

Once you have completed your list and feel you have nothing else you wish to add to it, you should now compare your list with the list I have presented in the back of the book (see page 202). This list was gleaned from the many lists I have received from my clients over the years. As you compare your list with this one, carefully note which of the characteristics on your list match or are similar to the ones I have listed. Does the model ideal friend list contain any other important characteristics you might now wish to add to your list to make it more complete? If so, add them to your list now. As you compare your list with the model, also decide whether you have any items on your list you now wish to modify or delete so that it fully satisfies your definition of an ideal friend. Once you have completed this review and editing process, you will have a good working draft of your ideal friend list. A rule of thumb for testing the completeness of your ideal friend list is to ask yourself if you could imagine living a truly happy and fully satisfying emotional life without ever again experiencing one or more of these elements (like loyalty, fun, or patience perhaps). If you can't, please be sure to include them.

In taking the time to complete this part of the exercise, you have allowed yourself to undertake a serious examination of what we human beings believe we fundamentally need from each other, and for ourselves. You may never have given yourself the opportunity to think about this topic so deeply before, to discern what really is best for someone else and what really is best for you—what they need, and what you need—in such a complete way. Now you have, and now you know.

Of course it is still possible that you missed something on your ideal friend list. Even if you did, you can always add it to your list at a later time. Remember these characteristics are ideas. They are tools for optimizing your mood and emotional adjustment. As with any tool, you should be looking for the ideas that work best for you while getting rid of the ones that don't. Think carefully about which ones you keep; not only will you own these thoughts, these thoughts will influence and control, your thinking. Editing and refining how you think is a highly important and adaptive, life-long process that can help strengthen your personal happiness over time.

Discussion and Meanings of the Ideal Friend List

Now that you have carefully thought through the question of what constitutes an ideal friend, it is time to look at the deeper

106

meanings and purposes that this part of the exercise is intended to reveal. You might be amazed at what we discover here. As we begin this discussion, please have your list in front of you. We will now go over five major topics to this discussion.

Topic One - Some Revelations About the Ideal Friend Exercise

You have a good sense about the nature of human nature. Having gone through this exercise hundreds of times now, I am struck by how well my clients are able to get in touch with the nature of human nature. Let me explain. To answer the question of what an ideal friend is we must first examine ourselves. We must get in touch with who we are and what we need; we must get in touch with what we all are and what we all need. To decide what an ideal friend is or should be we need to know who we are and what we are about. In looking at these Ideal Friend Exercises, I am always impressed by how thoughtful they are. The content is always genuine and intimately reflective of the human condition, so mindful and true to the ways we need and desire to be treated and treat others. For this reason, I often find myself saying, "Your list shows me you have a really good sense about the nature of human nature." In that regard, I wish you were sitting here with me right now. I am confident that I would be saying the same thing to you right now.

Ideal friend lists show stunning agreement. I also never cease to be amazed at how similar the contents of the Ideal Friend Exercises are from one person to the next. I could almost say to you, "If you have seen one, you have seen them all." Over and over again, the same qualities appear on these lists. Often, the exact words or phrases are used. The lists have been so identical at times that I found myself thinking, "Could this person have copied from somebody else's list?" Teasingly, I have asked, "Are you people colluding with one another in the parking lot?" I certainly know that we humans often have trouble agreeing with one another on a lot of things, but when it comes to the ideal friend, we seem to have no trouble at all. We all seem to agree.[7] This truth in numbers is consoling, and it is the major reason why I feel I can trust and rely upon using this information as much as I do.

The exercise seems to be revealing a universal truth about us. Knowing how hard it can be at times to decide on the right direction in our lives, I am encouraged by what I see here. When I ask people what they need, I am likely to get dozens of different answers including a lot of "don't knows" and "not sures." Granted we are all different in some ways, but if we were all so different at the core, determining the right emotional direction for our lives would be like aiming at a vaguely defined moving target. Good luck hitting it! Happily, the information we gather here most definitely shows that when we are asked the right question, we really are able to clearly see what we human beings need emotionally. Importantly, there is universality here; at the core,

---

[7] How do our perspectives on an ideal friend compare to those of other cultures? Cultural background may create some differences; however, I suspect we would find substantial agreement on what constitutes the ideal friend across cultures due to the universal nature of human needs. Cross-cultural studies with the Ideal Friend Exercise would be illuminating.

we all share the same basic emotional needs and wants. Remember this always.

As we go about our search for the important answers to our happiness, it is encouraging to realize that we do not have to reinvent the wheel. We do not have to spend our lives aiming uncertainly at a mercurial target as we search for these answers. Rather, it appears that we all have this internal compass pointing toward a common emotional destination that each of us ideally wants to reach. The beauty of the friend exercise is that it gets us to see what we really need most of all. A clearer sense of true north emerges. And given that so many of us seem to be pointing in the same direction about where emotional true north lies, I am led to believe that we are getting at something invariant and universal about ourselves. Examined through the prism of the Ideal Friend Exercise, we are able to see the fundamental things we all need; the things that bring about the state of well-being all of us long to have.

Trust in your implicit wisdom. I am so impressed by how "right on" my clients' ideas are about being an ideal friend that I often ask playfully, "Gee, did you do this exercise before?" I know of course that almost none of them have, at least not in a formal way, but I want them to see something. I want you to see this too. I want you to see the implicit wisdom you have about what is most meaningful to your life, to see that the ideals you put on your list reflect this core wisdom. They did not come from me; they came from you. This wisdom is yours. In doing this exercise, you have allowed yourself to make this implicit wisdom

109

become explicit. Trust in this wisdom; it is your wisdom. I trust it.

Wisdom of profound importance. I believe the qualities you have put down on your ideal friend list—the qualities you would want from an ideal friend—express wisdom of profound importance. Let me repeat, wisdom of profound importance. I do not make this assertion casually, and you might be questioning whether I am being sincere. I am. I want you to see that what you sense to be true about our human nature is true and enormously important. In the next section of this discussion, we will look at the deeper meanings and importance of your implicit wisdom.

Topic Two - The Blueprints: Six Important Meanings of the ideal friend List

As I talk to you about the important meanings of the ideal friend list, I want you to imagine existing in a world where all of the ideals you expressed about an ideal friend were ones that you could experience each and every day: acceptance, fun, support, caring, a sense of being deeply valued, trust, someone there whenever you need them, forgiveness, patience, understanding, doing things that interest you, love, respect, etc.—all of the things we long for. Keeping this image in mind and sensing what you would feel like, let's examine some of the important meanings of the ideal friend list.

A blueprint for love. The meaning of love can be a slippery slope. People seem to think about, use, and act upon this word in a myriad of ways. If I had to try and extract its true meaning from the popular culture, I would surely get lost. But, the Ideal Friend Exercise provides an excellent prescription for fulfilling the most important meanings of love. Put simply, treating someone in a manner consistent with the ideal friend list seems to convey in action what love truly is—whether we are speaking of romantic love, maternal love, paternal love, fraternal love, or what have you. The friend list offers a definition of how to love that seems almost beyond improvement. The ideal friend list is already paying some rather handsome dividends. But wait until you see the rest.

A blueprint for nurturing. Put simply, can you think of a better list of ingredients for nurturing a human being than those on your ideal friend list? When I reflect on it, it seems to provide all of the right ingredients. I do not know what else I would add. As we go about our lives as friends, lovers, parents and more, it would be nice to keep this blueprint for how to nurture clearly in mind. We need look no further. We will be mindful of how to nurture.

A blueprint for esteem. This is another extremely important meaning that the ideal friend list affords. In common parlance, the meaning of esteem is not all that clear. Do we really understand what it means? Do we understand esteem well enough to be able to explain to another how to have it, show it, feel it, or live it? How can we teach self-esteem if we are not clear on what it is or how to bring it into existence? The vacuous notion that self-esteem means "feeling good about yourself"

111

simply begs the question; it does not answer it. Once again, the friend exercise provides an important answer. By defining what esteem really is in a performative sense—in actions that show esteem—it captures the thoughts and behaviors that convey esteem most meaningfully. It shows us the actual qualities of thought and action that make us feel esteemed. Since esteem is a key concern for many, knowing what it really means is something worth knowing.

A blueprint for emotional security. I realize that by saying that the ideal friend list is a near perfect blueprint for creating emotional security, I am making another pretty tall claim. But I am ready to stand by this claim. Think about this with me: when, for instance, a child is raised with these nurturing ideals, wouldn't that child feel more secure? When you are treated in this manner, do you not feel more emotionally secure? The nurturing elements of the friend list are also the roots of our emotional security. Considering how important our emotional security is to us, we really do need to understand how to go about getting it. Reflect on the elements of the ideal friend list. By fulfilling core emotional needs, each and every one contributes in one way or another to our security. Each ideal strengthens well-being; a strong state of well-being defines a state of security. But there is even more. I want to point out two other hugely important benefits that the Ideal Friend Exercise offers us.

A blueprint for happiness. Perhaps I am saving one of the best meanings of the list for last. My work with the Ideal

Friend Exercise has convinced me that it also gives us the blueprint for genuine happiness. Once again, I would like you to imagine existing in a world where all of the ideals you expressed on this list were ones that you were experiencing fully. Would you not be feeling happy, truly happy? Not the kind of intermittent happiness we get from getting Things or doing Things (reminiscent of Computer Road?), but a more intrinsic and genuine kind of happiness. A kind of happiness you can't really buy at a store or keep after taking a vacation. When we over-depend on these effervescent Things for happiness, we get caught on a treadmill where we have to keep doing more of these Things, or our happiness soon evaporates. Discovering how to experience all of the nurturing qualities of our ideal friend is to discover the path to true happiness. There is one more extremely important meaning we will look at next.

A blueprint for emotional well-being. I wanted to save the best for last. Can you imagine any better blueprint for emotional well-being than one enriched with all of the nurturing ideals we have ascribed to our ideal friend? I can't. From research in hedonics, a branch of psychology that deals with pleasurable and unpleasurable states of consciousness, we know that even great wealth, fame, or winning the lottery produce only a temporary uplift in happiness. Their effects are usually situational and transient. Counting on them for our happiness and emotional health is like playing the emotional lottery. The odds are slim, and the benefits fleeting.

With the ideal friend list, we have a blueprint for well-being

113

that is intrinsically grounded in our emotional needs and realities. It contains the real experiences we emotionally long for. Authored from within our hearts, the veracity of its nurturing and emotionally uplifting values is apparent to us. It is totally authentic. That makes it a very good blueprint indeed. The unresolved questions are, "Can we make well-being endure? Can we make our happiness and well-being intrinsic and lasting, or must we forever stay on our emotional treadmills, playing the emotional lottery while chasing our illusory hopes of attaining these ideals?" The answer is, we can make lasting happiness, and by doing so, we can free ourselves from the makeshift emotional substitutes that are needlessly exhausting, chancy, and ultimately futile.

Topic Three - The Sometimes Paradox

After reading all of these high aiming promises I just made, I would not be too surprised if you were thinking that the good doctor is sounding more and more like a total dreamer. As I go through this exercise with my clients I have certainly been asked, "Where do I find this ideal friend you are describing? Perfect friends don't exist in my world." This is a fair question. However, they don't realize that they are actually making my point for me. We rarely do find all of these characteristics in one person. Perhaps we could experience more of the sought after bliss and contentment we long for if the world we lived in surrounded us with near perfect friends, family members, and lovers who had nothing better to do than always be at our side, nurturing us in every way. But in the real world we know this doesn't happen. At best, we have the support and company of good friends, families and lovers only some of the time. But there is a big problem with *sometimes*.

The trouble with sometimes is that sometimes we get loved, and sometimes not. Sometimes we may get esteemed, sometimes not. Sometimes we will feel secure, sometimes not. And sometimes we will have well-being, but sometimes we won't. With these fluctuations, our hopes for more enduring contentment go straight out the window. And if sometimes doesn't happen very often, we can get in real emotional trouble. I will talk more about the emotional problems that develop from inconsistent nurturance in Topic Four below.

If you really think about it, all of the nurturing ideals on the ideal friend list are necessary and important for well-being—not just some—all! In fact, that is why you put all of them on your list to begin with. As soon as even one is missing, just one, things start to go bad. For example, if you do not have somebody there when you need support, well-being begins to dissipate. If you don't feel accepted or valued as you are, or feel you can trust in someone, or feel there is someone there to listen to you, or someone who cares about you, happiness fades into concern and sometimes disturbance. Remember what is at stake here: our happiness, our security and our well-being—matters of great importance to us. Having them only some of the time really isn't enough. Unfortunately, many of us believe that this is reality and that this inconsistency is all we can expect from our imperfect world. We settle for a level of diminished happiness and is created by an inaccurate, self-limiting belief.

Think of the nurturing qualities in the ideal friend list as links in a "chain of nurturance": each link in a chain must be sound for the chain to be whole. If any link is broken, the vital chain of nurturance is broken. In fact, our emotional well-being is sustained only when this chain remains complete and unbroken. But many of us live in a world where the chain of nurturance is weak, incomplete, or broken and our well-being is fluctuating and compromised. We need a healthy state of mind to endure, but if we only receive the nurturance we need to sustain it sometimes, we will not be able to sustain well-being. For many people, the idea of enduring happiness seems paradoxical: how can they have lasting happiness if they only experience the nurturance that brings happiness about sometimes? They are snared in what I call the "sometimes paradox." As you read on to the discussion about the Chinese proverb, you will find an excellent strategy to resolve this seeming paradox.

Topic Four - Some Telltale Signs that the Chain of Nurturance is Weak or Broken

There is a direct connection between our level of nurturance and our state of emotional well-being. If we encounter mild to moderate life stress and our chain of nurturance is relatively intact, we might only experience mild feelings of distress such as irritability, annoyance, worry, moodiness, or nothing at all. Overall, our level of well-being will stay pretty high. However, if the chain of nurturance is more compromised, life stressors will have a greater emotional impact on us. Our well-being will dissipate and we will show certain telltale signs and symptoms that our ability to nurture and cope is insufficient. When we are unable to give ourselves the healing emotional supports we need, one or more—sometimes all—of the following telltale emotional trouble signs will likely be present:

Low self-esteem. A person will tell me that they have insecurities about being liked or that they have problems with self-esteem. They may be experiencing difficulties in relationships and feel worried that these sources of nurturance and support may be at risk. They have uncertainties about esteem, externally and internally, which offer clear indications of problems with the chain of nurturance.

Anxiety. Anxiety is another telltale symptom, but why? Anxiety results from uncertainty about important concerns. As uncertainty increases and the stakes get higher, anxiety also gets higher. When the chain of nurturance is uncertain, the most important resources for meeting our needs for love, security, and emotional wellness are in doubt. The core elements for anxiety are in play and the telltale sign of anxiety appears.

Depression. Suppose we feel more certain about the threats to our well-being. We feel the channel for nurturance is permanently blocked as we become increasingly negative about our life and future. Perhaps we have concluded that we just aren't good enough and never will be good enough. Or maybe we are thinking we have never really known true happiness, and never will; we are wondering, "What's the point to all of this?" Very often these are the kinds of thoughts depressed people have. As we grow more certain that the channel to our happiness is permanently closed off, the telltale sign of depression emerges. Negative thinking may worsen, merging into a general feeling that "everything is bad," or that "nothing matters anymore." Depression is a telltale sign that the chain of nurturance is not functioning properly.

Compulsion and Addiction. Similarly, while meant to afford emotional relief, compulsive behaviors such as excessive drinking, working, and eating or ritualistic checking, cleaning, ordering, hoarding, and hand washing are in fact problematic substitutes for not knowing how to nurture and soothe ourselves correctly and calm our anxious thinking. When we see signs of addiction or compulsive behavior, we are also seeing difficulties with nurturance. When we lack the kinds of nurturance we need for well-being, we will feel emotionally needy. To cope, we may also find ourselves looking for some alternatives to make us feel better or prevent us from feeling bad. Some activities can help us feel better like taking walks, reading, or working in the garden. Other activities can be problematic. Over reliance on food, shopping, alcohol, or work to feel better can lead to compulsion and addiction. These problem behaviors tell us the chain of nurturance is broken.

Topic Five - The Chinese Proverb

There is an ancient Chinese proverb by the Taoist founder, Lao Tzu, which suggests a better path to resolving the "sometimes" paradox. You may already be familiar with this proverb: "Give a man a fish and you feed him for a day. Teach a man to fish and you feed him for a lifetime." This proverb gets to the essence of what we must do to resolve the sometimes paradox and experience enduring well-being.

If we rely on the world around us for our nurturance, we are "fed for a day." We feel happy when those around us feed us the nurturance we need, but we depend on them too much. When we depend on others around us for our emotional comforts, our well-being waxes and wanes depending on what they do for us. Our happiness is situational and intermittent; our base of emotional security is unstable. Our inability to be more self-nurturing and self-reliant leads us into repetitious reliance on the world around us out to satisfy the emotional hungers that lie within. Enduring happiness is beyond our reach.

To enjoy enduring well-being and our own true happiness we need to know how to "feed ourselves for a lifetime." We must learn to rely more upon ourselves to take care of our own emotional needs and be responsible for our own happiness. We must complete the chain of nurturance from within, giving ourselves the ability to be our own ideal friend. When we gain this ability, we create the mindset for more lasting happiness and well-being within us. We no longer have to go through life caught up in the self-defeating game of emotional lottery.

Some Points to Remember

Your Ideal Friend Exercise is your wish list for how you would like to be treated and how you would like to treat others. You have this important wisdom about what is emotionally best for you. Your list contains the nurturing elements that form a chain of nurturance. Together they give you a blueprint for esteem, security, happiness, well-being and more. By developing a self-nurturing mindset that is guided by these elements, you will be opening your life up to lasting joy and emotional health.

Study Guide Questions

1. The Ideal Friend Exercise provides a blueprint for esteem. What other important emotional blueprints does it offer?

2. Why should you think of your ideal friend list as a "chain of nurturance?"

3. What are the four "telltale signs" that usually indicate the chain of nurturance is impaired or broken?

4. How does the Lao Tzu's proverb apply to the issue of nurturance?

5. Why are the elements of the Ideal Friend Exercise so important for your happiness and emotional health?

6. Explain the meaning of the "sometimes paradox."

7. We really seem to agree about what constitutes an ideal friend. Explain why.

9

Building Block 9: Creating the Mindset for Emotional Well-being

Loving yourself is not selfish; it is essential for true happiness and sound emotional health

Your ideal friend list (and the model ideal friend list on page 202) contains the essential attitudes and behaviors for nurturance and well-being. When you regularly care for yourself in this fashion, you are highly self-nurturing. Through a commitment to give yourself these essential emotional resources each and every day, you make your peace and happiness deeper and more continuous. When you need acceptance, you are there to offer it; if you want forgiveness, you find a way to give it to yourself. You are resolved to be there for you—not sometimes, but always—to be kind to you, to be helpful and supportive, to be positive and so on. Together these are seen as defining values in your relationship with yourself, as well as others. Live by all of the empowering and healing ideals on your list and, you live by the mindset for emotional health and happiness.

But first I would like you to determine how self-nurturing you are now. Do you treat yourself as you would your ideal friend? Ask yourself how diligently you do each of the things on this list *for yourself,* up until now. **Rate yourself now on each element on the ideal friend list.** This assessment will give you a clearer picture of your self-nurturance baseline.

In completing these ratings, please use the following rating system for each item: Give yourself a five if the item is one you do for *yourself* (not somebody else) "always or almost always." For example, if you think you are always or almost always patient with yourself, rate yourself a five. If the item is one you do for yourself "most of the time or a lot," give yourself a four. For example, "I am usually caring toward myself," or "I keep trust with myself (trustworthy) most of the time," would get a rating of four. If the item is one you feel you do "sometimes or somewhat," rate it a three. If the item is something you would do rarely or very little for yourself, rate it two. For example "I rarely deeply value myself," or "I value myself very little," would both get a two. If your answer is "never or almost never" to a particular item when it comes to doing it for yourself, for example if you are never or almost never supportive of yourself, you would rate it as a one. If you think you fall in-between two numbers, say between a two and a three, you can use a decimal point to give a rating that is in between the whole numbers such as 1.5, 2.5, etc.

As you complete your ratings, please remember that you are rating how well you do these things for you, not for others! I offer this caution because people are inclined to think about nurturance in terms of how they act toward others. They often forget that they are supposed to be rating how nurturing they are toward themselves and begin rating how well they treat others. ***Please use the ideal friend list on page 202, or the list you prepared, to complete your ratings now.*** Once you have completed your ratings, you will be able to pinpoint the behaviors on the list that you do very well and the ones that need strengthening. You will have the opportunity to work on those needing improvement a little later on.

Frequently, the ratings I see on the ideal friend list cluster toward the middle of the scale. I will see a lot of twos and threes, maybe a few ones and fours, very few fives, if any. Individuals with these profiles certainly have some self-nurturing abilities, but their abilities need improvement. Perhaps they need to learn greater self-acceptance or patience. Maybe they admit to being "too hard on themselves" and need to work on being less demanding, more self-forgiving.

Some individuals, on the other hand, answer "rarely" or "never" to most of the items on their ideal friend list. The necessary emotional learning for self-nurturance has been greatly compromised in these individuals. Due to the lack of self-nurturance, they will usually show some of the telltale signs (symptoms) of emotional disturbance such as depression, self-esteem issues, etc.

If we examine our histories, we can usually identify some of the reasons why we did not become more self-nurturing. Sometimes the explanation will be obvious; there was parental neglect or abuse, or too much external control. Sometimes the reasons are subtler, such as being caught up in a family culture of perfectionism, being overly concerned about what others think, or learning to avoid emotional conflict within the family at the expense of expressing our true feelings. Or perhaps our inability to self-nurture is due to the most prevalent cause: we simply weren't taught how to do it very well.

Many parents are not self-nurturing because, like many of us, they never learned how. Not that our parents wouldn't want to show us how to be self-nurturing if they could, but they simply can't show us how to do something they themselves never learned how to do for themselves. As children, how can we learn what is not being taught? Unfortunately, we often don't. Equally problematic, it appears that formal education has done very little to address these emotional learning deficits in the people I have worked with over the years. It is little wonder that so many of us struggle with emotional neediness and a fruitless search for well-being.

Whatever the reasons are that may have limited emotional learning in your life, there is really no reason why you can't acquire it now. You may have some doubts about this: people frequently express doubts in the beginning, such as, "I have a feeling that this will be really hard for me to do." If you are having doubts, remind yourself now that gaining this knowledge now will be easier than you think and far easier than continuing down life's path without it.

Not only is learning how to become more self-nurturing straightforward, it is the kind of learning which actually makes

126

you feel better as you go. In this respect, learning self-nurturance truly will feel much easier than staying on an emotionally bumpy road. But the real proof that self-nurturance can be learned readily comes from seeing my clients, one after another and week after week, master these skills with relative ease. As they do, their doubts give way to increased self-nurturance and their telltale signs and symptoms are replaced by marked improvements in how they feel emotionally. I am confident that this is what will happen for you as well!

Despite these words of encouragement, the prospect of learning how to treat yourself in all the ways of an ideal friend may seem overwhelming to you. The thought of becoming proficient in every one of these self-nurturing behaviors could seem daunting. But the good news is: you won't have to learn each quality separately! You may need to strengthen a few of these qualities, but I am willing to bet that you see significant improvement in many, if not all, of these self-nurturing behaviors without having to specifically work on each and every one of them. To be clear, I am not claiming a modern day version of alchemy here, where we magically turn lead into gold. Rather, it just so happens that there is a *shortcut* to self-nurturance and well-being that will speed your journey. Before taking this shortcut, I want you to see the reasoning that makes this shortcut possible and the *emotional blind spot* that keeps so many from seeing this path to ongoing nurturance and well-being.

Having the Right Motivation for Intrinsic Well-Being

As you can see now, by becoming self-nurturing—an ideal friend to ourselves—we can give ourselves the emotional resources we need for enduring happiness and intrinsic well-being. So why don't we just do it? What holds us back from treating ourselves the way we say we would like to be treated by an ideal friend? To move forward, we first need to see what may be holding us back.

Let's try looking at the question from the following perspective: suppose I were to hand you a twenty dollar bill and ask you to give me back three ten dollar bills in change. Unless you were having a bad math day or feeling exceptionally generous, I think you would decline. Why would you decline? You would decline because you would see that it's not worth it to you. Ordinarily, we will give what we think something is worth, not more. Value determines worth. When we value something, we are willing to give something for it. It is only natural that the more we value something, the more we are willing to give, the more we will strive to cherish and take care of it. When it comes to us, the same rule applies. We only give ourselves what we think we are worth. In order to self-nurture well, we must see our worth—we must learn to value and love ourselves!

You will recall that one of the elements on the ideal friend list is that we *deeply value* our ideal friend as they deeply value us. This element, as it turns out, is the real cornerstone for emotional well-being. It is only when we deeply value and love ourselves that we truly want to care for ourselves as we would an ideal friend. If we have learned to truly esteem and value who we are, self-nurturing feels normal and right and we will want to do it consistently; not doing it feels neglectful if not abusive. We have the natural desire and motivation to look after ourselves with dedicated caring and consistency—the same way we would want to look after Little Sara.

When we do not value ourselves enough, the essential motivation for self-nurturance will be lacking and we will not be nearly so inclined or able to give ourselves what we need. We will find ourselves situation-bound with our happiness generally confined to the chanciness of the emotional lottery. Well-being will be intermittent at best. We may have one or more of the telltale signs that our chain of self-nurturance is broken such as anxiety or addictive behavior. Additionally, we will be more needy and prone to codependency. We will need other people and other Things to give us what we don't give to ourselves.

My favorite phrase regarding this state of affairs is, "Please love me, because I don't know how." Love becomes need. "I love you" may really mean "I need you to love me." The essential point is that you must learn how to deeply value who you are because this is what gives you the critically important motivation to self-nurture correctly and promote your emotional health and happiness. You must always be there for you!

Happily, there is this shortcut to becoming more self-nurturing. The shortcut lies in realizing that you already know how to display most of the qualities on our ideal friend list. You know how to nurture. You already have experience being a good friend and nurturing to others. If you are like most people, however, you may be more accustomed to being a good friend for others than for yourself. Your nurturing efforts may be significantly more outbound than inbound. Balance provides the answer. You must value and care for yourself as you would others whom you cherish. Once this balance is correct, you will find that giving yourself the nurturance you need comes about pretty quickly—you are already practiced in using these habits for the well-being of others. Having the knowledge of how to be an ideal friend to others within you gives you this shortcut.

Why is it that we so often miss this shortcut? To use the ideal friend list on ourselves, we have to value and care enough about ourselves to be self-nurturing, and here is where the blind spot comes into play. I have asked my clients to tell me why they were not more self-nurturing in the past. Some simply don't know or say that they just never learned how. But many have said that they felt they would feel "selfish" or "egotistical" if they loved themselves, or treated themselves in such a special or caring way. This thinking is one of the main reasons for the blind spot. It seems many of us somehow learned to think that it is good to nurture and love others but it is selfish to nurture and love ourselves. When we have learned to think that loving ourselves is selfish, we lack the motivation to self-nurture and wind up needing other people and Things to nurture us. We look outward rather than inward. Given that we are often brought up to think in ways that promote this blind spot, it is not surprising that so many of us are emotionally needy and find the path to emotional wellness difficult to see.

Now, examine the ratings on your ideal friend list. How self-nurturing are you? Whose job has it been to nurture you, yours or theirs? What rating did you give yourself on "deeply value who I am"? Do you see a correlation between the rating for how much you value yourself and the other ratings? More than likely there will be one. Very often people rate "deeply value self" at two or three and a lot of their ratings on the other elements cluster around this score. Their ability to self-nurture is hampered. See if low self-value (self-love) has been holding you back from treating yourself the way you wish to be treated—it usually is the culprit. If it has been, low self-value is a problem that you can eliminate, allowing you to move forward. We will examine this subject next.

Seeing the Ideal Pathway to Intrinsic Well-being

Intrinsic emotional well-being occurs naturally following an optimal sequence of events: The sequence begins when we receive proper love and nurturance from our parents as children. When we are loved unconditionally and within healthy boundaries, we experience and internalize a deep sense that we are loveable, that we are deserving of feeling this way about ourselves. When we are esteemed unconditionally, self-esteem comes to us naturally and we learn to feel deep value for ourselves. When we believe we have true value, we are naturally motivated to self-nurture. Our self-nurturance, in turn, propels

131

us to strengthen and broaden our happiness and security. In this way, the optimal pathway to intrinsic emotional well-being is completed.

Frequently, this optimal pathway is not what we experience in early development. The result is that we do not know how to love ourselves correctly. We lack the necessary motivation to self-nurture and, thus, we are unable to create sustained well-being. True, you cannot go back to your childhood and ask that the sequence be done over correctly. But you can do something else, here and now that will truly fix this problem once and for all and you will know the process of how you got there. Not only will your happiness be firmly secured, you will have a complete understanding of how you created this emotionally healthier version of you! I think you are now ready to learn how to be truly self-valuing and have genuine self-esteem —not by acting selfishly or egotistically, but by learning genuine esteem for yourself—the same kind of esteem we would wish for Little Sara.

How to Deeply Value Yourself

Once again the solution to deeply valuing yourself lies in your thinking. What you think about yourself determines how you feel about yourself. Your thinking determines how much you value yourself. First, we will look at what is usually wrong with our thinking in this area. After we have done that, we will go over a straightforward, failsafe method for correcting it. As you recall, we carry all kinds of cultural scripts in our heads that

132

shape how we view Things, including how we view ourselves. Some people naturally like and love who they are. If you were very, very lucky, you might be one of them. But if you were, you probably wouldn't be reading this book. As mentioned before, many of us think that loving ourselves borders on selfishness and egotism. Unfortunately, this thinking takes us completely out of the running for intrinsic self-esteem and sound emotional health. Unable to embrace self-love, we ask, "What did I do to deserve my own unwavering esteem" or "Isn't love and nurturance of me a job better left for someone else to do, like my parents or spouse?" We instantly deny ourselves the necessary motivation for lasting self-nurturance and emotional balance. Whatever the case may be, each of us needs to replace these ill-founded, toxic scripts that cripple self-esteem and well-being with something better. We need positive and healthy thinking that properly motivates self-nurturance and well-being. In short, our thoughts must be self-esteeming.

Carefully consider the reasoning in the following syllogism: The extent to which you value yourself will determine how well you nurture yourself, and how well you nurture yourself will determine your level of intrinsic well-being and emotional health. This is a truism. Just as eating, sleeping, and breathing are essential to your physical well-being, loving yourself is essential to your emotional well-being. Deeply valuing or loving yourself should never be thought of as inappropriate or undeserved. To the contrary, thinking about yourself in this way is essential. It is something we all must do because our well-being absolutely requires it!

Just as blind-spot thoughts can stop us from truly loving ourselves, there are other incorrect ways of thinking about our esteem that can also be problematic. For example, many people confuse performance and achievement with self-esteem. In some cases, their self-esteem is almost all about success and performance, about how well they are doing. They don't actually have intrinsic self-esteem; they have what I refer to as "performance-esteem syndrome."

Here is the problem with performance-esteem as a substitute for intrinsic self-esteem: when we tie self-esteem to what we accomplish, we tie our emotional welfare to it as well. Our well-being fluctuates with our performance, and our well-being becomes situation-bound. When we have good days and perform well we like what we have done and we like ourselves. But when we are not performing well, we shut off the esteem and our well-being ebbs. Our happiness is intermittent, switched on and off by depending on performance-based esteem. Performing well should be important to us, but we should not sacrifice our joy and happiness on its altar. When esteem and well-being hinge too much on performance, sustained well-being is impossible. Performance-esteem is not, and should not be, a substitute for your self-esteem.

Striving for excellence, high performance, and a value-driven life are noble goals, but falling short in these pursuits is never a good reason to diminish self-worth and well-being. As we will see, there are healthier and safer ways to deal with our failings and shortcomings. If we only love and deeply value Little Sara when she is good and performing well, she will never experience lasting happiness and security. What does not work for her, will not work for you either.

Thinking which co-mingles self-esteem with how others feel about us also creates problems. Caring about the feelings of others and how they feel about us is understandably important, but remember: how others feel about you is not intrinsic self-esteem, it is other-esteem. The esteem of others is rooted in them, not you. The extrinsic esteem of others is a poor substitute for real self-esteem. Over-reliance on the esteem of others fosters dependency and loss of personal control over your own well-being. While it is arguably best to have both sources of esteem, it is essential that you have your own. Self-esteem is something you must provide yourself! The esteem of others is never a good replacement for your own self-esteem.

If we think that we should only value and love ourselves when we have done something to earn or deserve it, we endorse another bad idea for our emotional welfare. Using this earn-it to deserve-it thinking fosters compulsivity and needlessly restricts the necessary flow of self-nurturance for our well-being. Relaxing becomes difficult because you feel like you always have to do something in order to feel good about yourself. A classic example of this is the Type A personality. People with Type A personalities are always in overdrive. They are overly competitive and work constantly—try to get one of these people to relax during the first few days of a vacation! They always feel like they have to work or be productive in order to feel good. Their self-esteem and well-being are conditional: both are tied to their work output and performance. Eternally busy bees, they seem to be driven by the mantra, "good, better, best; never let it rest, 'til the good is the better, and the better is the best." If Little Sara is ever to have any real hope for peace and happiness, she must avoid taking this path, and so must you!

If our accomplishments, other people's opinions of us, and this "earn it to deserve it" mentality should not be used as the primary basis of self-esteem, then what should be? In short, your self-esteem should be rooted in unconditional love for yourself—the exact same thinking that convinces us to deeply value and love Little Sara for who she is. She is loved when she is studying and she is loved when she is chasing a butterfly. Even more importantly, she is loved when she is doing absolutely nothing at all. If you'll recall Building Block 4, we determined that loving her in this way greatly increased her chances of flourishing.

In order for you to flourish, you must follow the same path. By making your self-value deep and unwavering, you provide strong and steady motivation for self-nurturance and make certain that the foundation for your happiness is resilient and enduring. This is not to say that you should ignore or minimize the value of your efforts and accomplishments. But instead, use these resources to fortify your feelings of self-worth, never as replacements or prerequisites for it.

Many people are concerned that loving themselves will lead them to be too self-centered. What I observe is that people who do not love themselves enough are usually more needy and often burden others with their neediness. Loving yourself quiets the neediness. When we properly love and look after ourselves, we are less burdened with our own needs and our actions are less likely to be self-centered. Since we have more of what we need, we are more able to give without needing to get. For many people, the fundamental problem is not that they will become too self-centered by loving themselves, it is that they are too other-centered and self-neglecting because they do not love themselves enough! Loving ourselves is not hedonistic or self-centered: it is a prerequisite for personal happiness, good mental health, and loving others. The answer lies in creating a proper balance of love for self and others.

Your intrinsic well-being is directly related to your ability to esteem and nurture yourself. It helps if you think about the relationship between genuine self-esteem and intrinsic well-being this way: when self-esteem or self-value is very low, intrinsic well-being will be very low as well. When well-being is at its lowest levels, we enter the *perishing zone.* In this zone, we struggle to find even brief glimpses of happiness. We also have the telltale signs and symptoms of disturbance that go with this diminished state of well-being.

Intermediate self-worth gets us into the emotional middle ground, the *languishing zone.* In this zone we experience periods of emotional wellness, but they are not continuous. Happiness comes and goes and the telltale symptoms of under-nurturance appear from time to time. Many people are stuck in the languishing zone. Their lives are dotted with ups and downs—a mixture of event-based happiness and unhappiness with problems like low-grade depression or excessive food/alcohol consumption often entering the picture. They often rationalize their acceptance of intermittent happiness by telling themselves, "This is reality; life isn't supposed to be a bowl of cherries." Sometimes their happiness bounces further up or falls further down, however it usually comes to rest in this intermediate level of well-being. Unfortunately, many live out their entire lives in this languishing zone.

We can do far better than this! We absolutely can experience a deeper and more enduring state of emotional health and happiness. However, to attain this level of well-being, we must first learn to give ourselves the love and nurturance we need. Only when we have learned these things can we bring our well-being and happiness to its highest levels, and only then are we able to stay in the *flourishing zone*. This is where you are heading.

How to Deeply Value Our Imperfect Selves and Eliminate the Last Hurdle to Enduring Self-Esteem and Well-being

How often I have heard, "I'm a lot harder on myself than I am on others!" I am convinced that mental health practices around the world would be far less busy if we weren't so hard on ourselves. Being too hard on ourselves causes serious problems with our emotional welfare and this is why I asked you about it in the Ideal Friend Exercise. Not only do we fail to self-nurture enough, we also tend to be too hard on ourselves to boot! This is a very bad (feel free to read as 'terrible') combination for emotional well-being. When we mistreat ourselves by being too hard on ourselves, we seriously violate the fundamental necessity of self-respect and weaken our own well-being. We must learn to avoid being too hard on ourselves because this behavior is emotionally harmful and completely contradicts the ideal of being a good friend to ourselves.

When we are too hard on ourselves, our failings and shortcomings can trigger toxic levels of guilt, blame and self-recrimination. Some punish themselves with negative thoughts to the point where it would be called verbal or emotional abuse if it were said out loud. They justify this negative behavior by claiming that their self-admonishments correct their behavior and help them to become better human beings. If they were less harsh, they feel that they would let themselves get away with things. Their implicit thinking says, in effect, "I must be hard on myself, even shame and punish myself at times, to correct my failings and be a good person." These seem like noble intentions of course; people are tough on themselves in order to be good people and deserve their own esteem, and this all sounds almost reasonable. Unfortunately, this underlying thinking is not sound at all. In fact, it needlessly drags us down and is emotionally toxic.

Of course, we should strive to behave well. However, trying to compel proper behavior through self-deprecation causes more harm than good. Harsh self-admonishment does little to ensure real change in behavior. Genuine self-esteem is a precious emotional asset; demolishing it by belittling yourself is never a good idea. No matter how noble the purpose, when we bear down on ourselves with harsh self-judgment, blame, guilt, and recrimination, we seriously harm our self-esteem and ourselves. Instead of changing and improving our actions or really fixing anything, we now have two problems: first, we have wasted time and energy engaging in self-criticism and have done nothing to correct the original problematic behavior, and second and more concerning, through our blame-and-shame thinking, we have unwittingly damaged our self-esteem and well-being. In a very real sense, we have turned against ourselves, condemning our selves rather than our behavior. In fact, if we think like this, we never learned how to maintain good self-esteem to begin with.

Remember: being angry with ourselves never changes behavior; it just damages the relationship we have with ourselves! Severe self-criticism makes us feel bad about who we are and depletes both self-esteem and positive energy for changing behavior. On the other hand, positively encouraging needed behavior change, and being resolute about changing it, is what really helps us change behavior.

In short, being too hard on yourself is not the best way to go. It causes problems with your esteem and it does not work very well. Being a good person, acting responsibly, and encouraging personal accountability are all important pursuits, but there are better ways to achieve them without damaging your self-esteem and emotional wellness. First, you should always remember to distinguish yourself from your behavior because they are not the same thing. It is OK to disdain behaviors you disapprove of, but don't disdain yourself. I don't really like Little Sara's behavior when she hits her brother, but I still love her. I certainly will let her know when her behavior is bad, but I don't want her to think she is bad. If I fail to make this distinction, I can damage her emotionally. Similarly, when you fail to make this distinction, you damage yourself.

I am not offering an "E-ZPass" here for skirting around bad behavior. We must still aim high and hold ourselves accountable. But we need to approach correcting and improving our behavior in a different way, instead of blaming and punishing ourselves for our failings and shortcomings. Rather than waste all of this energy damning and damaging ourselves in negative and unproductive ways, we should redirect all of it toward a clear and constructive plan for corrective action.

As an incentive for teaching ourselves to behave correctly, always keep in mind that the natural rewards and benefits that come from behaving consistently with deep value and esteem for ourselves and others far exceed those of self-deprecation. We are not better-off blaming ourselves for overeating, or drinking too much, or smoking. Instead, because we love and care about ourselves and because we don't wish to act in ways that harm us or others, our energies are better spent on creating a serious plan for correcting problematic behaviors and on steadfastly keeping a commitment to this plan. We attack the problem, not ourselves. It's a lot easier to honor such commitments when you have learned to honor (deeply value) the person you are doing this for —yourself.

By approaching our failings and shortcomings in a constructive way, we preserve well-being and free-up more positive energy for correcting these problems. Loving yourself gives you good reasons and good energy to behave well and correct failings. With this approach, we maintain personal and moral accountability, we address our human failings efficiently and constructively, and we come away with our self-esteem and well-being still intact. By following this approach, you will promote a healthier and more effective adjustment to life.

Having read through the previous discussion, you are already on your way to correcting any blind spots that block your ability to deeply value and properly love yourself. Now, all that remains is for you to put the correct thinking in place. The process is straightforward. First, you will read through the six-step plan outlined below. I have provided many of the details and you should fill in the rest where appropriate. Once you have become familiar with these steps, simply do exactly what your plan says to do. Here is the six-step plan guide I would like you to work with:

(1) **Who** will be in charge of this plan? This will be you.

(2) **What** will you do? You will teach yourself a new thought pattern that will help you value yourself correctly. A revised thought pattern designed to improve thinking and behavior that I term a corrective cognition. You will think to yourself, "I am fully committed to deeply value (or love) myself unconditionally, forever." If you prefer, you can choose to write up your own corrective cognition, just be sure that the thinking clearly conveys a true sense of unconditional love for yourself.

(3) **Where** and **when** will you do this? I would like you to provide these answers. Think about times and places where you will be most likely to use your corrective cognition such as in the shower, on the ride to work, over coffee, when you end a phone call, etc. What works best for you? Be sure to write these ideas down. They are part of your plan.

(4) **How often** will you do this? I would like you to set the target goal, but I would like you to consider engaging in this new thinking at least ten times throughout the day.

(5) **How long** will you do this? Probably a few weeks or until you feel you are ready to believe this new way of

thinking forever.

(6) **Evaluate** to make sure you are remembering to do the specified number of corrective cognitions every day. At the end of each day, check to make sure you did them. If you forgot a few, you can catch up right then. Be sure you do this step!

In case you are wondering whether this six-step plan actually works, I can answer unequivocally 'yes' because I have watched it work over and over again. The only time it has not worked is when somebody didn't follow the plan—not surprising! Will it take up much of your time? Considering that it takes six seconds or less to say or think the corrective cognition presented above, and considering that you would do this ten times a day, we're looking at roughly 60 seconds. *That's only one minute a day for a life-altering change that will allow you to have intrinsic well-being!* Seems like time well spent to me.

I left a few details for you to decide upon on your own with this plan. That's because it is important that you take ownership over this important change. You may know best what works for you. You can use the corrective cognition I have listed above if you like—it is one that works well. But if creating your own thought pattern that conveys enduring worth and love for yourself is something you would like to do, and if you think it would help you, then by all means do it. Just be sure your revised thinking makes your self-esteem and respect complete and unwavering. As an example, a young mother told me she likes to say to her daughter, "I love you to infinity and beyond," every night when she says good night to her. Eventually, she decided she would say the same thing to herself. It's a good example of a corrective cognition because there is no mistaking its meaning, or depth of sincerity. A good friend endorses this idea: "I will love you forever; I will like you always."

After you have decided on your corrective cognition, you need to fill in the rest of your plan, namely where and when, so you make certain you manage to think this thought at least ten times a day for three weeks or more. I would like to go over this a little more here. Regarding when and where—think about creating cues that will serve as reminders for you, such as when you are in the shower, or when you are brushing your teeth, or each time you use the stairs. My clients have successfully used all kinds of cues to prompt them to remember: post-it notes, placing the corrective thought on their screen saver, using the stairs, a purple yarn bracelet, a modified password such as "value-me" or "value-me-5" (ideas associated with the highest level "valuing" on the Ideal Friend Exercise), one person decided to engage the corrective cognition when driving, each time he turned right! I thought this was a little over the top, but the truth is that he achieved outstanding results by using this cue.

There is a very good reason why I recommend you evaluate your plan on a daily basis. By completing this evaluation at the end of each day, you can make sure you are putting your plan to work. If you forgot to do the new thinking a few times or altogether that day, you can still follow through now, completing corrective cognitions on the spot. If necessary, you can revise certain details in your plan to make certain that you are successful. Being accountable to yourself promotes learning and increases the likelihood that the desired change in your thinking will come about more quickly. As you go through this process and see yourself make life-altering changes in your behavior, you will deepen your confidence in your ability to control your emotional destiny and personal happiness.

In the beginning, many say they feel strange or uncomfortable saying the corrective cognition to themselves. It is not wrong or unusual to feel like this at first. It's normal. More than likely you have never told yourself how important you are, or how much you deeply love or value yourself. Because this new thinking is so different, it usually does feel weird for a while. However, as you continue to rehearse the corrective cognition, you will become used to this new way of thinking. In two or three weeks the thought of loving yourself will seem more natural.

Another common concern is whether or not this process will really work. While it does work, having these doubts is also normal. Realize, however, that you have already come a long way in your thinking: by now you see the benefits of having greater happiness and emotional well-being, and the logic of how and why you need to deeply value yourself. If we were talking about taking a vacation, it would be as though you had already decided where you wanted to go and purchased the airline tickets. You may not be there yet, but you have made real progress towards

146

reaching your destination. Similarly, you realize the importance of learning to love who you are and its necessity for your emotional welfare, and you have decided to do something about it. You may not be there quite yet, but you are already well on your way.

Now, over the next several weeks, commit to carry out your six-step plan for deeply valuing yourself. Be sure to do it daily and remember to evaluate at the end of every day. Make this your primary focus: keep rehearsing the corrective cognition that deepens self-esteem. Do your best to remember to do it each day, but don't get down on yourself if you forget. Just correct the problem by continuing with your plan. Usually within a week or two, this new thinking will start to feel familiar and more normal to you. This is a good sign. After three or four weeks, your belief about deeply valuing yourself should be well-established. You will have opened up the pathway for self-nurturance and well-being. *During this period, I highly recommend that you go back over this material again to reinforce and strengthen what you have learned. These sections are the heart of this book and it is essential that you know them.* As you engage and reengage your new corrective cognition, closely monitor and reinforce your progress in accepting the belief that you fully value and love yourself. When you reach the point where this new way of thinking feels correct "most of the time," or better yet, "always or almost always," you have successfully implemented a hugely important change in your thinking, by giving yourself the correct foundational belief for continuing self-nurturance and well-being. This new belief is precious and well-deserved. It is a belief never to be lost or put aside.

Some Points to Remember

Many of us aren't conditioned to treat ourselves like we would a special friend or to self-nurture correctly. We operate with blind-spot thinking. We fail to see that we should be the one most responsible for our own esteem, love, emotional care and happiness. Sometimes, we believe that loving ourselves is selfish or egotistical. For these or other reasons, this job is left for others to do, or left undone. The main problem is that we lack the necessary motivation to love and care for ourselves, and in turn, flourish emotionally. We postpone loving ourselves while we continue to work on being the person we think we must become to deserve this love. All this does is postpone happiness. Now, by learning to deeply value yourself, you will be giving yourself this intrinsic motivation, the natural desire to forge the chain of nurturance and wellness from within. You will truly want to care for yourself the way you need to be cared for, and this shortcut will make it easier.

Study Guide Questions

1. Why is it so important to deeply value and love yourself?

2. There is a "shortcut" to self-nurturance. Explain this.

3. What thinking causes the "blind spot"?

4. See if you can finish this syllogism: The extent to which you value yourself will determine how well you....

5. Performance-esteem or the esteem of others is not a good substitute for self-esteem. Why?

6. Explain the "languishing zone."

7. Describe what a "six-step" plan is.

10

Building Block 10: Strengthening the Habits for Self-Nurturance and Well-being

When we self-nurture well, we have more to give others and less we need from them

Very often, the simple act of thinking correctly about our self-worth—deciding to love ourselves unconditionally—automatically increases our willingness and dedication to be self-nurturing. Once we really do value ourselves, we want to do the best we can to nurture and care for ourselves. Chances are that this is happening to you right now, but it is probably best that you actually look and make sure that it is. You can check by rating yourself again on each of the elements of your ideal friend list. If you see that these ratings have increased, your new thinking is working and already helping you to nurture yourself better. As your motivation to properly care for yourself builds, you begin to act in more caring ways toward yourself. Ideally, you want your ratings on the friend list to be at four (most of the time), or even five (always or almost always) if possible. The reason you want them to be as high as possible is that your intrinsic happiness will reach its highest level when you are consistently supplying yourself with each of these highly important components of nurturance.

If some of your ratings on the friend list are still low—three or below—you should work to improve your self-nurturance in these areas. For example, you might need to review and refine your strategy on how to listen better, be more patient, or perhaps more forgiving with yourself. We will go over some examples of how to do this next. Some people aren't sure how to apply the friend list element, "have interests in common," to themselves. we'll be going over this as well. If your ratings show that you are already doing a good job self-nurturing in certain areas on the ideal friend list, please view the coverage of these topics as positive confirmation of your emotional learning. Remember: education can be new information or further confirmation of what you already know.

If you want to improve your ability to self-nurture in specific areas, you can use the "six-step" plan format that you learned about earlier. Following this six-step approach gives you a nearly failsafe method for thinking through and carrying out important changes in your thinking and behavior. In Step 1 (who), you make it clear that you will be the one responsible for making the change in your thinking or behavior. In Step 2, you decide what new ideas you will be thinking or doing. Here, the point is to come up with one or more good ideas that are consistent with the objective of the self-nurturance element, and to be sure that you make them specific enough so you know what is required to carry them out. For example, if your self-nurturance objective includes becoming more positive towards yourself, your idea might be to think of a complimentary thought such as, "I really got a lot accomplished today." Your compliment need not be performance-based, however and you might simply decide to think, "I like who I am."

Staying with the six-step plan format, you will also need to decide where, when, and how often you would like to practice and reinforce this new behavior. Taking the time to figure out these small but important details will greatly increase the likelihood that the changes you want will actually occur. You might notice that I left out how long. For all of these wonderful and healthy self-nurturing habits, I think you will want how long to be forever! Of course, you always want to evaluate these efforts. The daily check helps you to determine if you are following through correctly. Finally, subsequent ratings on the friend list elements will allow you to gauge the benefits you are realizing through these self-improvement efforts.

Now we are ready to look at some example plans that will help you to improve your habits of self-nurturance on selected elements of the ideal friend list. These plans focus on examples you can use, namely Step 2 corrective cognitions and actions, to strengthen various habits in your chain of self-nurturance. The other steps in the six-step plan formats for improving these habits should be self-explanatory, and they are usually best decided by personal preference and practicality. The habits that we will address here are: listening to yourself, self-acceptance and forgiveness, being loyal to yourself, being patient with yourself, and having interests in common. I am including this last behavior because many of us have difficulty seeing how to apply the idea of "having interests in common" to ourselves.

Listening to Yourself

There is a good reason I chose to address this habit first. I put listening first because, when it comes to self-nurturance, listening to yourself is what you should do first. Listening to yourself is the essential first step in initiating the chain of self-nurturance. It allows you to hear (pay attention to) your feelings, to see if you are happy, sad, bored, lonely, excited, angry, tired, or maybe a little frustrated. You can't look after what you don't notice. Only when you take time to notice and hear your feelings by listening to them, are you able to really find out how you are doing and offer the kind of nurturance that would be best for you. In listening to yourself, strive to follow the same healthy mindset you would follow if you were really listening to Little Sara. You would want to listen to her caringly and regularly because her emotional health and happiness depended upon it, and so you will want to carefully listen to yourself because yours does too. In fact, when we don't do this, we emotionally abandon ourselves. We either depend upon others to listen to us or we run the risk of becoming emotionally run-down and symptomatic through the self-neglect of not listening to ourselves. In short, in being an ideal friend to yourself, strive to be a good listener to yourself—it is one of the most important things you can do to improve your self-nurturance and well-being.

Here are some ideas for how you can become a good listener to yourself: first, select a quiet time and place where you can listen to yourself without a lot of distractions. Having this solitude helps you to focus in on what you are feeling. Adopt the mindset of listening to yourself with genuine interest and caring —and without judgment. You will be more comfortable and you will be more likely to express your true feelings if you approach yourself in this positive fashion. You want to make listening to yourself a helpful and positive experience. Caring and acceptance help to make this important habit something you will enjoy and repeat. When we are too critical and hard on ourselves, we make listening negative and unpleasant—listening to how we feel becomes something we would rather avoid. It is important to use a gentle hand and be compassionate with yourself.

Try asking sincere questions such as, "How are you really feeling?", "What's been on your mind?", and "Has anything special been happening?" Ask, then listen—really listen—without judgment. Acceptance feels better than harsh criticism, so make listening to yourself a *friendly* experience.

Pay close attention to your feelings, making sure you really listen to how you feel. If you hear good things, you can respond by savoring your happiness. Listening to how you feel can be fun as well as helpful in other ways. If you find yourself feeling sad, you can offer caring and concern. If you are experiencing problems, let yourself know you are there and ready to help. Remember, this kind of empathic listening is where self-nurturance begins.

Now, please take some time to reflect upon the process and mindset you have previously used when listening to yourself. After reading this material, what changes, if any, would you like to make to improve your listening? If you see ways that will improve how you listen to your feelings, incorporate them into a six-step-plan. Be sure to prepare a complete plan that includes regular, daily listening, as well as times and places for this activity. As always, evaluate what you are doing each day to make sure you get the changes you want.

Self-Acceptance and Forgiveness

Due to their interrelation, I think it is appropriate to examine self-acceptance and forgiveness together. That is, if we were always self-accepting, we would rarely, if ever, need to forgive ourselves to begin with. Although we may occasionally have good reasons to disapprove of our behavior, we would not blame and condemn ourselves for how we behave if we were always self-accepting. If we were self-accepting, we would continue to love ourselves, even when our behavior was wrong or harmful. Instead of condemning ourselves, we would condemn our wrongful actions and resolutely set about correcting them. Thus, if we avoid harsh self-blame to begin with, we won't have to waste so much energy trying to repair its damaging effects through forgiveness. After all, this energy would be far better spent actually correcting our faults and shortcomings.

156

Here then are ideas that you might consider using to help create a better balance between your needs for self-acceptance and forgiveness:

> ➢ Decide to make unconditional self-acceptance a core belief.
> ➢ Think about it in much the same way you think about deeply valuing yourself.
> ➢ Remind yourself that you are fully accepted daily.
> ➢ Identify wrongful behavior that warrants correction.
> ➢ Resolutely commit to correcting wrongful behavior.
> ➢ Identify and eliminate any thinking that has given you reason not to accept yourself.
> ➢ Reject wrongful actions and behavior, not yourself.
> ➢ Practice self-acceptance and accountability rather than self-blame.
> ➢ Realize that blame and shame never correct wrongful behavior, only correcting does.
> ➢ Remind yourself that you will always have your own acceptance, even if someone else chooses to withdraw his or hers.
> ➢ Be mindful that self-acceptance is a prerequisite for true well-being.

If some of these eleven ideas are not part of your mindset at this time, try using them to become more self-accepting or less self-punishing. To make improvements in these areas, prepare a six-step plan that will help you reach your desired goals.

Put what you are learning into action. As I have said to you before, *knowing it* means *doing it*. Knowing *about* something or telling yourself you "know the right thing to do" does not mean much if you still don't do it. It is as if there are two levels of knowledge: The first is being aware of the information. The second level is when you ultimately embrace and act upon this information with consistency. When a person with an alcohol problem says, "I know I drink too much," yet continues to drink too much, how much do they really know? If you read what is discussed in this book, you know *about* it. If you *do* what is recommended in this book, you really *know* it. Please make sure you take an active approach in knowing these techniques—allow yourself to experience the rewards of actually doing them!

Being Loyal to Yourself

Being loyal to yourself is another critical link in the chain of nurturance: lasting emotional wellness depends upon it. You must be able to count on yourself to self-nurture correctly if well-being is to be maintained. *Conscientious and consistent self-nurturance brings about enduring happiness.* Upholding your commitment to care for your emotional needs and happiness conscientiously and consistently is what "being loyal to yourself" really means. We become loyal to ourselves by reliably looking after our emotional needs and preserving our emotional welfare through proper self-nurturance. There is no one else who can or

158

should be doing this job for us. Loyalty to yourself also means relying on you to honor and stand by your feelings and values. Being able to voice your emotional truth and assert yourself when necessary promotes good emotional self-regulation and helps protect mental health and well-being. It is good to be assertive about your feelings, needs, and values; it is being loyal to yourself.

If you need to work on restructuring your thinking so that you will be more loyal to yourself emotionally, consider endorsing ideas such as:

> ➢ You deeply value yourself when you are loyal to yourself.
> ➢ Being loyal to yourself means you will be there for you.
> ➢ You give yourself security by making yourself someone you can count on. Being loyal to yourself gives you this security.
> ➢ By being loyal to yourself you will take on the job of looking after yourself seriously, and you will do it well.
> ➢ Your happiness and emotional health absolutely depend upon you being loyal to yourself.
> ➢ Being loyal to yourself helps you to be conscientious about self-nurturance.
> ➢ Self-loyalty enables you to stand up for what you feel and believe in. Saying what you feel occurs more naturally and feels like the right thing to do.

➤ Ignoring your feelings and emotions is neglectful and disloyal to your well-being.

These ideas can be incorporated into your mindset by using them in Step 2 of your six-step plan for increasing emotional loyalty. Try writing one now.

Being Patient with Yourself

Many of us have difficulty being patient, especially being patient with ourselves. This impatience frequently accompanies being too hard on ourselves. There are a number of reasons why we may act this way, but none of them are very good for our well-being and happiness. Sometimes impatience derives from having set our expectations too high. An example of this thinking might be, "I should know how to do this, and I am quite upset with myself because I don't know how." The actual facts may be that we expected to know how to do something which we have never done before, and we are making ourselves upset and impatient about it. Should we be upset with Little Sara because she could not use scissors if she was never shown how? No, I think we would recognize that using scissors is a skill that requires time and patience to learn. Another situation many of us lose patience with and become upset about is when we face challenging circumstances that we can't seem to overcome. These situations often trigger frustration, anger and impatience. Sometimes it's a matter of intolerance towards our own or others' mistakes and shortcomings.

Acceptance, tolerance, and reassurance are tools to help us gain or regain patience and well-being when we face circumstances that lie beyond our immediate control. For example, we could think, "Becoming a good tennis player will take time and practice, and I guess I should accept the fact that I will mishit the ball a lot, especially in the beginning." In practicing tolerance, we can think, "They are somewhat loud, but they are just being children and having fun." Or while struggling with directions to program a new remote for the TV, we can reassure ourselves by thinking, "I can probably get this remote to work, I just need to work with the directions a while longer."

If patience is not yet your virtue, the following ideas should be helpful to you in developing a six-step plan:

> ➤ Decide to make patience a priority in your thinking for how you treat yourself and others.
> ➤ Remind yourself that it is more realistic to expect what you are able to do rather than what you are not able to do. Thinking this way promotes patience.
> ➤ Identify the circumstances that trigger impatience, and revise your thinking to be more accepting, tolerant, and reassuring.
> ➤ Look closely to see if perfectionism or being too self-critical may be at the root of your impatience. More often than not, these habits harm, rather than help, your emotional health and happiness.
> ➤ Remember that patient thinking is safe thinking.

> ➤ Realize that patience makes you and those around you feel better.
> ➤ Understand that patience is what Little Sara needs and what you need as well.

If you put some of this thinking into a six-step plan, you can teach yourself to be more patient.

Having Interests in Common...Yes, with Yourself!

Having interests or values in common with someone makes the connection feel more enjoyable. Activities that we are interested in are more reinforcing and valuable, more nurturing. So, how do you apply the idea of having common interests directly to yourself? You can do it in several ways. You can do it by encouraging interests in your hobbies, favorite sports, volunteer work, etc. You can do it by knowing what your interests and passions are and thinking about them. And, you can do it by making sure you take some time out of your life to pursue the activities that interest you.

If you think you could benefit by fostering more regard for your values and interests, now might be a good time to work on improving this self-nurturing habit. Below are some ideas that embrace nurturing your interests. Consider weaving them into a six-step plan to help you enrich your well-being.

➢ Inventory your interests, values and passions. Are there enough? Do they feel right or could developing others be helpful?

➢ Be active in promoting your interests and beliefs. Do you support yourself in this respect? If not, restructure your thinking so you have this support.

➢ Commit to giving yourself time and opportunity to engage in your passions and interests. What interests are you involved with now? Are there improvements you wish to make that will give higher priority to your interests?

➢ Little Sara gets bored and sad when she has nothing that interests her; she is happiest when she is interested in and enjoying her world. Be sure to take time to enjoy your interests too, in thought and in deed.

➢ Think of a change that you might make through a six-step plan that will allow you to have more satisfying involvement with your joys and interests.

Some Points to Remember

Self-nurturance is a mindset, a way of thinking that expresses regard for your mind and body. Your ideal friend list contains the essential ideas that guide this mindset. You can strengthen your nurturance and well-being by refining your thinking and habits of emotional self-care. By learning these habits of how to be an ideal friend to yourself in your daily life, you will bring about the proper self-nurturance that is needed for a healthier and happier life. The the ideas for six-step plans outlined above provide you with practical methods for improving these important habits. You can also use the basic outline of the six-step plan as a guide for improving other areas of self-nurturance. Building strong habits of self-nurturance creates the best foundation for sound mental health and more lasting happiness. As we close here, I ask you to please consider rereading this and the two preceding chapters (Building Blocks 8 and 9) to make certain you really know them.

Study Guide Questions

1. What do your ratings on the elements of your Ideal Friend Exercise tell you about your relationship with you?

2. Why is it important to evaluate progress on six-step plans on a daily basis?

3. Listening is first on the ideal friend list. Why?

4. Why should we look at acceptance and forgiveness together?

5. List three ideas you endorse to promote being loyal to yourself.

6. Explain what it means to have "interests in common" with yourself.

11

Building Block 11: How to Make Well-being Last

Happiness is felt when you choose to think safely about
something; happiness lasts when you care enough about
yourself to keep doing it.

Once you understand the thinking that begets lasting
emotional well-being, you must put this thinking into practice in
your daily life in order to sustain and realize all of the benefits of
what you have learned. Know means do, not "know about and
not do," or "only do sometimes." You really need to live by your
new skills and knowledge. By applying a self-nurturing mindset
everyday, you will be able to keep creating the personal joy you
desire.

We can learn how to have well-being, but we can also lose
it through lack of use. Like many other pursuits, initial knowing
of how something works is not the same as doing it and living it.
You must put this learning into practice—live it by doing it
everyday. In short, use it, or lose it. By being mindful about the
principles of self-nurturance, remembering to treat yourself as
you would Little Sara, and using what you have learned in your
everyday life, you take the final step for realizing enduring

happiness. You can now begin to live by the mindset that engenders happiness and well-being in yourself and others.

You have come this far; make sure you don't let yourself fall back. To prevent relapse, you must develop and follow a good maintenance plan that will keep you on track doing the things that make well-being last. Staying on track means living by the basic principles of self-nurturance that keep you feeling well emotionally each and every day. Having a strong maintenance plan is an essential step for making your well-being last. **Take some time now to write down a plan that will keep you focused on your well-being. In writing your plan, I would encourage you to:**

1) Assess how much and how often you are using the behaviors on your ideal friend list.

2) Review your ideal friend list each day and do checkups: rate and re-rate yourself on this list regularly.

3) Work up corrective plans for improving your self-nurturance where needed. Check your progress to be sure you are following through with implementing these plans.

4) Keep a journal or notebook so you can keep track of your planning, assessments, and progress toward

maintaining your nurturance and well-being.

5) Monitor your level of well-being regularly using the 10-point rating procedure we covered in Building Block 9.

6) Look for any patterns of unsafe, self-disturbing thinking and use the thought changing widgets to get unstuck from persistent negative thinking.

7) Review portions of this book and your notes from time to time to refresh and deepen your understanding of what you have learned. Pursue additional reading to help you to stay on your path.

8) Consider working with a counselor who has developed a practice model rooted in Positive Psychology or Cognitive Behavioral Therapy to gain additional help.

Below is a list of some of the key ideas for building happiness and emotional health that helped guide my thinking throughout this book. Remembering these ideas can also help you to maintain the right mindset for sustaining your personal happiness. As part of your maintenance plan, consider returning to this chapter and reviewing these ideas from time to time, so that they remain a firm part of your mindset for well-being.

➢ *Things* don't cause feelings, your thinking about Things does.

➢ You will not be able to self-regulate correctly if you mistakenly believe that your emotions are caused by Things outside of you.

➢ Remember to think, "It's not what he or she did that hurt my feelings, it's how I think about it that causes me to feel hurt."

➢ To feel well, you must first think well.

➢ When you think Things make you happy, you make happiness situation-bound. Then, you will only be happy when these situations occur.

➢ Be sure you are not thinking that Things have you down when it is you who is making yourself down about Things.

➢ Think safely; keep your thoughts on the right side of the road.

➢ Remember, the feelings of disturbance caused by unsafe thinking are not states to stay in; they are signals for you to take corrective action so that you can protect and preserve your emotional health and happiness.

➤ Maintaining a steady, self-nurturing mindset is the essence of staying happy and well.

➤ If you only want to feel happy sometimes, you only have to think well sometimes.

➤ Controlling situations is not a good substitute for learning how to control your thinking about them.

➤ When you change how you think, you change how you feel.

➤ Learning how to sustain happiness is nowhere near as difficult as living without it.

➤ You can and should choose what you think. Your thoughts should work for you, not the other way around.

➤ If you always think what you have always thought, you will always feel the way you have always felt.

➤ You do not get paid by the hour for making yourself feel bad with negative thinking, so don't beat yourself up for free.

➤ When you decide to make a big change in your beliefs by deeply valuing yourself when you had not done so before, you set a powerful motivation for achieving emotional well-being in motion. Old patterns of self-neglect feel noticeably wrong and get set aside; positive thoughts and actions about yourself and your life feel right to you and emerge in their place to bring about realignment with this new belief.

➤ To be happier, value being happy and engage in more positive thinking.

➤ Expand your stockpile of safe thinking and engage these positive thoughts regularly.

➤ Do what you believe in and believe to be good; you will feel happier.

➤ Strive to treat yourself as you would Little Sara. Make sure your thoughts and actions pass the Little Sara test. If they wouldn't be emotionally good for her, realize that they will never be good for you either.

➤ The love we are not given, we must learn how to give to ourselves.

➤ Waiting for certain Things to happen so you can be happy is a poor substitute for being happy while you wait for Things to happen.

➤ Other-esteem and performance-esteem are certainly important in their own right, but it is essential that you never view them as substitutes for your own intrinsic worth and self-esteem.

➤ Ongoing self-esteem and self-nurturance are essential for your emotional welfare.

➤ Look beyond your blind spot, loving yourself is not selfish or undeserved; it is essential for happiness and emotional health.

➤ Make deep, unconditional self-esteem an irrevocable covenant for the rest of your life.

➤ Remember, if you react with retributive self-blame to your human failings and shortcomings, you break the covenant of unconditional self-esteem.

➤ Disdain your poor behavior, not yourself. Use your vital energy for more resolute correction of these behaviors.

➤ Deeply value yourself today, and every day. Your health and happiness depend on it.

➤ Not loving yourself enough is the fundamental disloyalty that sacrifices emotional well-being.

➤ The extent to which you deeply value yourself determines how well you nurture yourself. How well you nurture yourself determines how much well-being you have.

➤ Psychotherapies that focus on our problems in the past fail to directly teach us how to think and feel well in the present.

➤ Strive to spend quality time with good friends, including yourself, every day.

➤ Let your understanding and caring for Little Sara guide your life: endeavor to consistently treat yourself and others the way you would want to treat her.

➤ Emotional wellness is not a part-time job; it is a fulltime commitment to a way of thinking and behaving that you live by each day.

➤ If you depend on others to nurture you, you will have well-being for today, but if you learn how to be self-nurturing, you will have well-being for your lifetime.

➤ You can only have real and enduring security when it comes from within, rather than from Things around you.

➤ Success in creating lasting well-being begins with valuing yourself and your personal happiness. Success in keeping it begins with making an enduring commitment to these purposes.

➤ When it comes to good friendship, most of us already know a lot—but we are usually a lot better at being friends with others than with ourselves.

➤ When we fail to self-nurture, friendships become "needships". "I love you" masquerades for "I need you… I need you to love me because I don't know how."

➤ Love begins where need stops. By loving yourself, you have something to give to another, rather than something you need to get from them.

➤ When it comes to your well-being, knowing it means living it. That is why follow-through and maintenance to help you keep living it are so important.

➤ By choosing to live by the elements of your Ideal Friend Exercise every day, you will have the blueprint for enduring happiness and well-being.

➤ Happiness is felt when you choose to think safely about something; happiness is lasting when you care enough about yourself to keep doing it.

Without fully realizing it, you may have sought nurturance and well-being from without rather than from within. Through your own experiences with the Ideal Friend Exercise, you see what all of us are searching for even more clearly. Now you know that by thinking about and treating yourself as you would an ideal friend, you can give yourself the enduring esteem, security, personal happiness and well-being you have wanted and deserve.

Some Points to Remember

Enduring happiness is not a matter of good fortune. It is brought about through living by and adhering to a self-nurturing mindset in your daily life. A good maintenance plan will reinforce the emotional learning you have acquired and help you keep your emotional welfare on track. To insure your success, a good maintenance plan is essential.

Study Guide Questions

1. Why is a maintenance plan necessary?

2. What steps do you intend to take to support your progress?

3. I list 45 key ideas in this Building Block that helped guide the writing of this book. Select three that seem especially meaningful to you. Why are they the most meaningful?

4. If you have not done so already, write down the maintenance plan you intend to follow now.

12

Building Block 12: Some Implications of Happiness and Well-being for Society

To possess emotional health and happiness, first
we must be taught how to think and feel well

In closing, I would like to share a few additional thoughts I have about the importance of having sound emotional learning and intrinsic happiness in our lives. First and foremost, I stand in agreement with those in the Positive Psychology movement who suggest that we shift the focus from mental illness to mental wellness. It is my view that many emotional problems and disorders including anxiety, depression, and addiction arise from and are worsened by our failure to properly teach mental wellness. It would be more productive to view most of them not as medical disorders but as learning-based behavioral problems, problems rooted in the way we have learned to think emotionally. Treating these problems by simply medicating them, or by only working on the symptoms associated with them, will not fix what ultimately causes them. Helping individuals learn how to think in ways that enable wellness offers a more direct and promising way to address both the causes and solutions of such problems.

Mental health is more than being free of symptoms or diagnoses; it is having the ability to think and behave in ways that sustain emotional well-being. This is where we need to aim.

What must be done to change the status quo? The stakes are high. A life without much happiness or personal joy is not much of a life. Happiness and emotional resilience correlate directly with sound emotional and physical health, as well as with productivity, civility, and other important aspects of human behavior. On the other hand, when we have not learned how to practice emotional wellness, the telltale signs of emotional disturbance are apparent. Millions of lives are affected, taking an enormous toll on our families, workplaces, health care system and society as a whole. To start, I believe that substantive "how to" education in emotional well-being should be a priority educational goal in our schools and homes. Knowing how to be emotionally well and sustain happiness are not intuitive—they are acquired ways of thinking that we must be taught and, in turn, teach.

Knowing how to think well emotionally has implications well beyond our personal happiness and mental health. It affects other important aspects of our lives as well, such as how we parent, how we behave as friends and life partners, and how we function in the workplace. Let's look first at parenting.

Parenting is among the most important jobs human beings do. Through parenting, our children learn many basic life skills—how to dress, feed, speak, socialize—skills vital to their physical survival and well-being over their lifespan. And when we show them how, they learn the right emotional language for feeling well. We can help them learn how to think and feel well about the world around them, about themselves, and self-nurture correctly so that they can competently look after their emotional welfare throughout their lives, and pass this knowledge on to the next generation. To acquire the right foundation for good mental health and well-being, our children must be taught how. It is of critical importance that we as parents possess the necessary skill sets so that our children receive the emotional education they need.

Our past experience is not a reliable educator for developing the necessary emotional skill sets. It depends upon what happened along the way and what emotional language we learned. A mindset that harbors elements of anger, worry, fear, self-doubt, or only performance-based esteem is not a mindset that will hold onto peace and joy, or one that will serve as a good role model for our children. The know-how of emotional well-being is not something that we can assume will come about on its own or be acquired after we have grown up. Unfortunately, many grownups have never really grown up emotionally. The mindset for happiness and emotional health is something that requires the right learning opportunities—it must be taught at home and through public education.

Positive emotional responses such as joy, laughter, and acceptance are not simply innate responses; they are heavily influenced by how we have learned to think about events and situations. When it comes to human emotions, our learning has a lot to do with how we feel. To feel proud, you must know how to think proudly about something; to feel hopeless, you must first be able to discern and endorse the absence of hope. As events occur, we tend to respond with the feelings that our thoughts generate. Learning also influences when, where, and how much we engage and express various positive and negative feelings. Hence, our moods are heavily affected by what we have learned along the way. Once conditioned, however, these thoughts, as well as the feelings engendered by them, tend to occur somewhat automatically, but that wasn't always the case.

From early childhood, experience begins to influence our emotional reactions. Experience shapes and defines much of the fundamental "emotional language" we use. For example, we didn't just land on the planet as worriers, optimists, "sad sacks," or "manly men" who never show their feelings. We learn to act these ways. We learn to be worriers, optimists, and "manly men" by intentional and unintentional parental guidance, as well as cumulative life experiences. We learn how to think and speak in English, we learn the language of mathematics, and we also learn the particular style of emotional language we use.

As children, we learned the languages we were taught, not the ones we weren't taught. This is also the case with our emotional language. We learned the emotional thinking and feelings we acquired as children and that we now have as adults. The emotional language we learn will be the emotional language we speak, i.e., the emotional language we acquired as we were growing up. It may or may not be the language that is best for our emotional welfare but it is the one we know. Our emotional language determines how we react emotionally and how we feel. If I learned how to see joy in life, I will know the language of joy and feel happier. If I was raised around worriers, I will more likely think and react like a worrier. Worry will be a distinctive part of my emotional language. If I learned my feelings were not all that important or unmanly, my emotional language may be one of silence. The emotional learning acquired in these early years can set in motion a life headed towards emotional wellness, a life of repeated ups and downs, or possibly even a life tormented by mental illness. As such, the emotional language we have learned turns out to be pretty darn important.

And this is why proper parenting and education in this area are so critical. If we are to provide a sound foundation for emotional well-being and mental health, as parents we need to know how to speak and teach the emotional language that promotes well-being. We need to have a good grasp of how emotions work and how thinking shapes both the good and poor emotional reactions we have to our world. We need to listen and respond to the emotional signals of our children with behaviors that foster optimum nurturance and well-being. We must be the ones to model happiness and teach feeling well so that our children learn how to feel well and acquire the right mindset for happiness and emotional resilience from the beginning.

As parents, we must be sure that our emotional language is the one we want our children to learn. They will copy what we do; they will learn what they see. If we want them to have healthy self-esteem, then we must have healthy self-esteem—only then can we show them how to think and behave as someone who has intrinsic self-worth would behave. If we think they should be self-nurturing, then we must be also. If we want our children to know how to think and feel well, we must know how to think and feel well ourselves so we can show and teach them these invaluable skills.

Knowing and living by a mindset that engenders emotional well-being is key. It helps us to teach and act as positive role models for our children. Keeping ourselves in an emotionally better place also has the benefit of helping us to act and react with more patience and nurturance during the day-to-day demands of childrearing. Fluency in the language of emotions is not only essential for our own happiness, as parents, it is equally important in helping our children to see, have, and learn how to keep their own peace and joy over their lifetimes.

Our capacities for emotional wellness also affect the nature of our relationships with friends and life partners. If we never learned how to be good at self-nurturing, we may struggle more with emotional ups and downs and be more emotionally needy. We may lean harder on others for this support. If our life experience has taught us that we should seek nurturance from others, rather than from within, we may be drawn to nurturing, caretaker types, who appear willing to do this for us. We will be inclined to resolve our own neediness through the nurturance of our friends and partners, using them to give us what we never learned how to give ourselves. But relying on others for our emotional well-being will never show us how to become emotionally complete; it actually prevents it. Leaning on others this way fosters emotional dependence rather than emotional independence.

Unbalanced relationships give rise to an interaction like that of a parent and child, rather than that of two adults. In these relationships, one person is emotionally underfunctioning while the other is overfunctioning. Over time, these relationships tend to spawn conflicts and resentments due to the inherent imbalance. Relationships of this sort are more susceptible to wearing thin and often end with the parties ending the relationship rather than taking steps to correct what is out of balance. When we are not proficient at creating our own happiness and security, we not only look for others to do so, we also hold them responsible for it. This need-based attraction in some relationships is what Bradshaw (1988) has termed "giving in order to get." Giving to get is one of the underlying dynamics of codependence. It is also one of the powerful dynamics underlying high rates of relational conflict and divorce in the United States. When we lack the ability to sustain our own emotional well-being, relational conflict and hiring and firing life partners often becomes our default solution instead of correcting the emotional lacking within ourselves.

Friendships and marriages have a better chance to sustain and flourish when both parties are emotionally self-sustaining. In these relationships, each person is able to bring a fuller measure of self-esteem and happiness to the relationship, rather than needing to extract these emotional resources from one another. These relationships tend to be resilient and enduring because the people in them are emotionally complete. People who are emotionally complete foster healthier relationships because they have learned how to make themselves more responsible for their own happiness rather than burdening others with this job. Adult love begins where neediness ends.

We take our level of emotional well-being with us wherever we go. It affects how well we feel, it affects how well we parent, it affects what we look for and how we behave in our personal relationships. It also affects how we function in our work life. I have heard it said that with a work staff of 30 people, you could give 28 the day off and the two codependent workers who agreed to stay would still do all of the work! When we don't have all that we need to be happy within us, we tend to use external Things as replacements. Work is often one of those Things. To get a sense of worth we may compensate by overworking in order to get the validation and approval that we ourselves lack. Under these circumstances, work begins to capture us like an addiction, becoming an uncontrollable pattern of behavior driven by neediness and the inherent deficiencies in our emotional well-being.

Ideally, our motivation for work should be not be propelled by these unmet emotional needs, but instead by practical considerations relating to our financial responsibilities, desires to engage in challenging work that we find rewarding and meaningful, and regard for our emotional welfare. When we behave with a strong foundation of emotional well-being, our motivation to work is tempered by a balanced pursuit of these ideals. It should not be a replacement for our self-esteem, or a testimonial to the fact that we are lacking in this area. Ideally, our work life should express a balanced motivation to better ourselves as well as the world around us.

Unfortunately, work does not match this ideal for many people. Work life is often unbalanced and there are several reasons why this happens. Some of these reasons are situational, such as job scarcity, changes in management, downsizing, etc. But sometimes, the problem lies within us. Sometimes, instead of approaching work as something we do to meet our financial needs and apply our abilities toward valued outcomes, our approach to work is one of redemption through self-sacrifice or laziness.

Work is out of balance because of an imbalance within us. If there is a pronounced deficit in our self-esteem and well-being, the way that we think and behave towards work can become another venue for imbalance. Work, like relationships, eating, drinking, and many other activities, gives us a way to fill in what we lack emotionally. When we are not good at validating ourselves, our need to seek recognition elsewhere is much greater. Work can become an addiction for those who routinely rely upon it to prop up their otherwise floundering egos and moods. Work is not only a financial necessity, but also an emotional necessity. When we use work to find our worth and let our jobs define us, we expend our energy maintaining this imbalance rather than correcting it. Work and performance-esteem become makeshift proxies for self-esteem. We need too much, so we give too much. In the end, however, we gain too little.

Deficits in self-esteem and self-worth can also have the opposite effect on how we approach work. Instead of using work as means to try to offset unresolved emotional needs, people sometimes head in the other direction. Because they don't have much self-worth, and they don't believe they deserve very much from this world, they don't try hard enough. Instead, they under-perform. They are not well-motivated to invest time in training or education that could advance their opportunities for a better job or career. They may work in jobs below their capabilities and avoid putting forth their best efforts in the work they do. Lacking a true sense of self-value and a balanced investment in work, they underperform by not trying hard enough. For these individuals, work often amounts to trying too little, gaining very little, and struggling too much. When we have these deficits in self-esteem and personal happiness, ducking out of work or diving into it are really not the ways forward. Rather, these are telltale signs that we need to move forward on another front. We must set about correcting the emotional deficits that lie within us.

If we hope to rear generations of people who possess the requisite knowledge and ability to be and remain emotionally well and happy, proper parenting is a critical part of the solution. Parents themselves must possess emotional wisdom to teach this

186

wisdom to their children and serve as good emotional role models. Entrusting the solution to hope and happenstance as we have done up until now, is not a credible solution. Far too much is riding on people knowing how to be emotionally well and happy. To meet these challenges, parents must be given opportunities to gain the emotional experience and education they need. Public education must step forward by making emotional learning a key component of the curriculum and reinforcing the learning that ideally begins at home. As I remarked earlier, I was instructed on many things during my extended formal education, but emotional well-being was certainly not one of them. Was your education any different? So much time was spent delving into practically every other topic but that of emotions and emotional well-being; so little time on something as important as how to be happy and well. Hopefully, these changes are coming now.

The rising popularity of Positive Psychology has ushered in a wave of intense interest in bettering our understanding of happiness and emotional well-being. Through these efforts, we are now building the base of knowledge we need to teach this subject in public schools. Along the way to becoming parents themselves, our children will learn about their emotional lives as well as how to build their self-esteem and maintain emotional health. They will bring this knowledge with them to improve the quality of their lives and better inform the next generation.

I want to wish you heartfelt congratulations. You have completed your journey here. With the knowledge you have gained, you have reached a new destination and a more joyful and satisfying life now lies ahead of you. You will not be letting circumstance fritter away your happiness and well-being. You realize that it is far better that you, not situations, control how you feel. Because you know this, you will be able to avoid lost moments, lost hours, and lost days—precious time stolen and wasted by self-disturbance over circumstance. Instead, by endorsing your mindset for happiness, you will be assured that more of your life will be a life that you treasure living.

Even though you may have been discouraged in the past, you now see that it is possible to find a happier life. Because so much of your sustained well-being depends on learning, you now understand that you can overcome the past by practicing and living by the knowledge you have gained for happiness and emotional health.

As you continue to enlarge upon the transformative effects of your own emotional learning, you will see how much you have altered your emotional destiny. By learning a new mindset for happiness, and by changing and improving the way you think and feel about yourself and the world around you, you have found a much better path. This new path has you well on your way to a more satisfying and joyful life. By making this choice, the power for happiness now lies within you.

You can now see that being optimistic or pessimistic, mentally well or unwell, are not simply conditions fated to you by your genes or history. Rather, your levels of peace, joy, and contentment are also things you can control, things you can create and sustain by the way you think and feel about yourself and the world. And, because you have now rooted happiness and well-being permanently inside of yourself, it will no longer be tethered to the vagaries of circumstance. Your happiness is yours and you are able to make it last.

You know that you don't have to stay stuck in unsafe, self-disturbing thinking that cripples emotional welfare and impoverishes happiness. You now have the choice and the resources to make your life, and the way that you think and feel about it, better for you. You have the widgets, the tools, and the mindset for self-nurturance—all of the building blocks for happiness. You have found the essential emotional wisdom that will allow you to experience more lasting happiness and emotional well-being over your lifetime.

You have discovered the importance of always treating yourself as you would an ideal friend. By treating yourself in this way every day, you will continue to bring the gift of happiness to yourself and to those around you. By choosing to nurture and esteem yourself unwaveringly, you have increased your ability to flourish and given yourself the opportunity for more enduring happiness.

I am confident that the changes you have brought yourself through reading this book will remain with you, deepen, and greatly enrich your life as you move forward. Let the successes you realized along your journey to a happier life be an inspiration for others. Along the way, know that you have my best wishes for your continued joy and well-being.

Now, please take a moment to complete the Reader Progress Evaluation and Feedback Form at the very back of the guide (page 210).

Study Guide Questions

1. Most of us learn to speak the emotional language that was spoken around us. Explain what this means.

2. Give an example of how the way a person was nurtured can influence his or her behavior as a parent.

3. How can low self-esteem affect a person's behavior at work?

4. Someone you know seems to spend a lot of time at work and has difficulty relaxing. What does this behavior suggest about their self-esteem?

5. Explain why mental health is more than the absence of mental illness.

6. Give an example of how the way we were nurtured as a child can influence our behavior as a parent.

What If I Need More Help?

This guide was written to help empower personal growth and happiness. Both you and I share this common pursuit. However, self-help is not always the complete answer. Sometimes the problems we face may be deeper and more challenging. Other answers must be found.

If you feel that you need further help, I strongly encourage you to seek it out. Your emotional health and well-being are important and there are many avenues open to you for help. You can obtain professional help from a psychologist, psychiatrist, or another mental health professional. Most health insurance plans have coverage for these services. Your family doctor can provide you with a referral if needed.

If you do not have behavioral health coverage through your insurance and are unable to afford professional help privately, you have other sources available to you through your county mental health system as well as community agencies. You can find these services in the blue pages of your telephone directory or by going online. Just remember, your emotional health and welfare are extremely important and you can always find more help if you need it. Care about yourself and pursue finding the help you need.

Acknowledgments

There are many to thank. I am especially grateful for the generous and capable editorial assistance of Lyn Alexander, Deirdre Kells, Lane Neubauer, Ph.D., James Petrilla, Michael Roszkowski, Ph.D., and Scott Spreat, Ph.D. The help and unwavering support of Pam Lione, who believes in my work and wants the message spread, has been the wind under my wings. I am equally indebted to my many wonderful clients whose emotional wounds and caring hearts helped define the resolutions within this work. Finally, with profound gratitude, I wish to express my appreciation for the love, support and superb editing provided by my wife Karin, my son Brian, and my daughter, Jaclyn, throughout this journey. A special thanks to Brian, whose talented and extensive assistance with the editing and design of this book contributed greatly to the quality and appearance of the final product. To all of you who helped enrich the experience and end result of this undertaking, I offer my deepest gratitude.

References

Bradshaw, J. (1988). *Bradshaw on: The family.* Florida: Health Communications, Inc.

Ellis, A. (2006). *How to stubbornly refuse to make yourself miserable about anything.* California: Citadel Press.

Ellis, A , & Harper, R. (1975). *A new guide to rational living.* New Jersey: Prentice-Hall.

Fredrickson, B. L. (2001). The role of positive emotions in positive psychology: The broaden-and-build theory of positive emotions. American Psychologist, 56, 218-226.

Proto, L. (1993). *Be your own best friend.* New York: Berkely Publishing Group.

Seligman, M. (2002). *Authentic happiness.* New York: Free Press.

Snyder, C. & Lopez, S. (2002). *Handbook of Positive Psychology.* New York: Oxford University Press.

Annotated Bibliography

In this section, I have listed and briefly summarized some selected readings that you might find of interest. The books listed include a number of important contributions to our understanding of positive psychology, happiness and subjective well-being. Interest in these topics broadens by the day so please view these works as only a sample.

Argyle, M. (2001). *The psychology of happiness*, (2nd ed). New York: Routledge.

This well-written text provides an extensive review and analysis of contemporary research on happiness and well-being. In this second edition, Argyle provides new material on the roles that humor, country of residence, and religion play in our experience of happiness. He also offers an explanation of why we have negative and positive emotions, and examines the relationship of satisfaction to happiness. Argyle also provides an excellent source of references for additional reading.

Ellis, A. (2006). *How to stubbornly refuse to make yourself miserable about anything.* California: Citadel Press.

In the fields of human sexuality and psychotherapy, the works of Albert Ellis have had a profound influence. He has been, and remains even after his recent death, one of the leading and most influential cognitive-behavioral psychologists of our time. In this book, Ellis carefully outlines and applies his thought changing techniques to a host of human emotional problems. As in numerous other works he has authored, Ellis argues that it is primarily our irrational beliefs, not situations per se, that cause our disturbance. This book presents specific techniques that teach us how to get rid of self-defeating ideation, use more rational thinking, and feel happier.

Ellis, A. & Becker, I. (1983). *Guide to personal happiness.* California: Wilkshire Book Co.

This is one of Ellis' classic books wherein he details the specifics of his Rational Emotive Behavior Therapy (REBT), his technique that shows us how to shed off the irrational thinking that impairs happiness. His methods have been highly effective and are widely acclaimed in helping people resolve a wide range of emotional problems and disorders. However, one can take issue with the implication that removing irrational, self-disturbing thought equates with being happy. Despite the title of this book, it seems Ellis may be telling us more about how to remove unhappiness, than how to create happiness.

Ellis, A. & Blau, S. (1998). *The Albert Ellis reader: A guide to well-being using Rational Emotive Behavior Therapy.* New York: Kensington Publishing Corp.

Encompassing more than 50 articles, this book is a compendium of Ellis' life work. The volume is divided into three sections: Part 1 covers his work dealing with sex, love, and marriage, and walks the reader back through his pioneering and often unconventional approaches to dealing with these important aspects of human behavior. Part 2 covers a wide range of topics relating to the theory and practice of REBT. This section offers a step-by-step discussion of his A-B-C procedures for modifying our self-defeating thinking and behavior by replacing our "irrational beliefs" with more rational thinking. Part 3 provides wide-ranging discussions about the use of REBT principles in education, psychology, risk-taking, self-acceptance, excessive religiosity, personality disorders, addictions, and much more. A great read on the breadth of Albert Ellis' work!

Fordcye, M. (2000). *Human happiness: Its nature and attainment.* Retrieved January 16, 2009, from http://www.gethappy.net/freebook.htm.

Fordcye gives a detailed analysis of happiness research but seems to interpret many of the findings from the perspective that our happiness is more determined by circumstances than by us. Even so, after combing through all of this research, he identifies fourteen principles we can apply to increase our emotional well-being. He believes that the human trait most responsible for happiness is "positive, optimistic thinking." He regards this element as the "royal road to happiness," as do I. Unlike Fordcye, I view optimistic thinking as behavior that can be improved upon by learning, not as a fixed personality trait. Fordcye holds back a secret in his writing that he reveals at the end of his book: he says happy people are people who have the trait of valuing or desiring to be happy (hopefully this is one we can cultivate as well).

Meyers, D. (1992). *Discovering the pathway to fulfillment, well-being, and enduring personal joy.* New York: HarperCollins.

This book is one of the better-written and more scholarly works in the field of Positive Psychology. Meyers maintains a healthy scientific skepticism throughout his extensive review of the research on happiness. His assessments of the findings frequently lead him to conclude that happiness is, for us, a slippery creature that often eludes our direct capture. Paradoxically, people often rate themselves as fairly happy—even happier than they actually are. Being financially well-off is no guarantee of being happy; situations that evoke happiness tend not to last and we seem to return to a lower "set point" on our happiness scale. No particular age or gender correlates with higher emotional well-being, while race and education level make little difference either. Even so, Meyers does find that states of mind are important to being happy, remarking that "positive, focused, believing attitudes make a difference" when it comes to personal joy. Another important factor for happiness is good self-esteem. Meyers points out, "Happy people like themselves." Happy people have a sense that they can direct their own lives and choose their destiny. (I would say these are cognitions worth cultivating and having!) When it comes to happiness and well-being, cultivating the right mindset matters.

Nettle, D. (2005). *Happiness: The secret behind your smile.* New York: Oxford University Press.

Another excellent read in the field of Positive Psychology. Nettle offers a good review of the literature, examining the connections between happiness, age, gender, income and marital status. Nettle suggests that our evolutionary history may have skewed our emotional response system to react more strongly to negative circumstances (for example, threats to our safety) than to positive ones. He thinks we are "wired" to survive by pursuing things that, once obtained, don't make us happy for very long. Our nature tricks us into wanting things that may not make us happy, because having these desires at one time helped us to survive. He also reviews promising research showing that we can reduce our unhappiness as well as increase our sense of well-being. Although not a practical guide on how to be happy, Nettle's work is clearly written and highly informative.

Proto, L. (1993). *Be your own best friend.* New York: Berkely Publishing Group.

At times I think I may not have written the book you are reading if it had not been for this inspiring book by Proto. His central thesis, which I strongly endorse, is that esteeming ourselves and relating to ourselves as a best friend enables us to achieve health and happiness. His book encourages and teaches us to be self-loving and self-accepting, and recognizes the importance of our thinking in bringing about personal change and happiness. As such, his work has inspired and reinforced the development of my own thinking about the essential cognitive elements for enduring well-being, especially the creation of my Ideal Friend Exercise. I am deeply grateful for Proto's seminal contributions to this field, and I would strongly encourage you to read his work.

Ramm, D. & Czetti, S. (2004). *The formula for happiness.* Xlibrus Corporation.

Compared to a number of the other "happiness" books on the market, this book offers more practical help for those seeking to improve their personal happiness. Ramm and Czetti present an interesting guide to increasing happiness, based on ten *core values* and four *core principles* that they view as bringing about true personal happiness.

Seligman, M. (2002). *Authentic happiness.* New York: Free
Press.

Martin Seligman, previous president of the American
Psychological Association and author of *Learned Optimism*, has
delivered a landmark book on the topic of happiness. As a
pioneering leader in the Positive Psychology movement, Seligman
recounts how psychology is finally moving away from its
longstanding fixation with mental illness, and taking greater
interest in discovering the nature of human happiness. His
review of research shows us that external circumstances are not
the primary driver of human happiness. Happiness is a belief; it
is rooted in optimistic thinking and it tends to gives rise to living
a happier, healthier and more meaningful life. Optimism,
gratitude, and forgiveness all help to engender a happier
existence. However, Seligman argues that there are other factors
beyond these that lie at the foundation of authentic happiness.
These are what he terms *signature strengths* and *virtues.* Only
when we carry out our life in accordance with these elements are
we able to realize authentic happiness. Not all agree with
Seligman on this point.

Model Ideal Friend List

Ratings*	Characteristics of an Ideal Friend
( )	A good listener
( )	Trustworthy
( )	Honest
( )	Caring (or Kind)
( )	Helpful and / or Supportive
( )	Loyal
( )	Dependable (or Reliable, or "There when you need them")
( )	Someone you really respect
( )	Forgiving
( )	Fun and/or Funny
( )	Accepting (or "Accepts who you are," or "Easy to be around")
( )	Knowledgeable (or Capable and / or Intelligent)
( )	Patient and/or Understanding
( )	Positive
( )	Share Common Interests / Values (or "Enjoy their company")
( )	Someone you deeply value (or Cherish, and / or Love)
( )	Non-judgmental (or not too critical or judgmental)
( )	Someone who is not too hard on you
( )	Easygoing

*Rating Scale for rating how much you are an ideal friend you to yourself:

5 = *Always / Almost Always*

4 = *Most of the Time*

3 = *Sometimes / Somewhat*

2 = *Rarely / Very Little*

1 = *Never / Almost Never*

Notes

Notes

Notes

Notes

Notes

Index

Reader Progress Evaluation and Feedback Form

Part 1

Dear Reader:

Please complete this page (Part 1) before and after reading this book. Answering these questions will help you gauge your progress in key areas. Estimate your level of self-nurturance, self-esteem, happiness, and emotional well-being using a 1- to 10-point rating scale (1= low, 10=high).

	My Level Before Reading This Book	My Level After Reading This Book
Self-nurturance:	[ ]	[ ]
Self-esteem:	[ ]	[ ]
Happiness:	[ ]	[ ]
Emotional Well-being:	[ ]	[ ]

Please give your percentages of safe and unsafe thinking after reading Building Block 2 and after completing this book.

Safe Versus Unsafe Thinking

Before		After Completing the Book	
% SAFE ( )	% UNSAFE ( )	% SAFE ( )	% UNSAFE ( )

Reader Progress Evaluation and Feedback Form

Part 2

My goal in publishing the guide is to provide practical information for improving personal happiness and emotional health. Now that you have completed your work with the guide, I would like to hear back from you about your experience. You can share a copy of your responses to Part 1 and Part 2 by emailing me at: thinkrightfeelright1@gmail.com or mail your reply to the address at the bottom of this page. Your answers will remain confidential.

Was this book helpful to you? Why?

Have you incorporated the message within this book into your daily life?

Do you have any recommendations for improving this book or a theme you would like to see developed as a chapter or entire book?

Thank you for your time and interest. You can mail your reply to:

Robert D. Isett, Ph.D.
Box 212
Fountainville, PA 18923